The Hyperactive Child

A self-help manual written by parents for parents who
want to help their hyperactive children get better.

THE
HYPERACTIVE CHILD

by

Belinda Barnes
and
Irene Colquhoun

THORSONS PUBLISHING GROUP
Wellingborough, Northamptonshire

Rochester, Vermont

First published 1984
Fifth Impression 1986

British Library Cataloguing in Publication Data

Barnes, Belinda
The hyperactive child.
1. Hyperactive children
I. Title   II. Colquhoun, Irene
618.92'9589   RJ490.B7

ISBN 0-7225-0883-2

Printed in Great Britain by
Richard Clay (The Chaucer Press) Ltd,
Bungay, Suffolk

6   8   10   9   7

ACKNOWLEDGEMENT

The authors owe a great debt of gratitude to Sally Bunday who founded the Hyperactive Children's Support Group and who is still actively involved in running the Group.

PUBLISHER'S NOTICE

While there is no risk of side-effects in following the self-help approaches suggested in this book, it is very important that parents consult their family doctors to ensure that no fundamental medical problems are being overlooked.

CONTENTS

FOREWORD

There is a right and a duty for all children who live in our developed, western world to receive an adequate education which should, in due course, allow them to take their place in adult society.

Mothers and fathers who have developed, through necessity, many stratagems to entertain and coerce their hyperactive child, to curb his excessive behaviour, must be aware of the difficulties experienced by the caring Reception Class teacher when confronted by her new pupil.

There are perhaps fifteen children in the Reception Class, all in need of attention, but the hyperactive child needs much more than his allotted time. He finds it difficult to concentrate, and fidgeting is second nature. His writing is poor because of lack of motor control, he is quite likely to be clumsy in the classroom and inadequate at games. At this point of low self-esteem the child can become very disruptive, often trying the patience of his hard-pressed teachers and classmates to the limit.

Teachers are becoming increasingly aware that the number of learning disabled children is growing at an alarming rate. No longer can we just pass these children off as 'naughty', 'badly brought up' or 'stupid', as has so often been done in the past. Here is a case where constructive help to alleviate the situation is desperately needed.

The HACSG is spreading a philosophy of hope to all

parents and teachers who come into contact with the group. Firstly there is the relief of knowing that you are not alone with your problems and secondly there is a wealth of practical knowledge, amassed by years of experience in dealing with hyperactive children, to draw on.

Hyperactive children who are put on a carefully planned diet of simple foods almost always improve on an all-round basis. There seems no predictable rule as to the form this improvement takes. For some the effects are dramatic and immediate, for others slower and more painstaking. As general health improves so fewer school days are lost for minor ailments. Parents are rewarded with a calmer child and the teacher is encouraged by a child who can now sit still long enough for teaching and learning to take place. Slowly, lessons are learned and manual techniques mastered. With the improvements come moments of success and breakthrough which are immensely rewarding for the young person who has known mainly failure to date. Following each success comes the motivation to achieve even more and the process of education begins to take its due course towards the production of a well rounded, integrated adult.

Having taught hyperactive children for some years it seems to me only right that all concerned with the future of these children should have the opportunity to read this book, to understand what may have gone wrong with the finely balanced machinery of the child's system and hopefully set all children back on a better path towards health and well-being for the future.

Valerie A. Ehlers
Specialist Remedial Teacher

INTRODUCTION

In centuries past children's health was threatened mainly by infectious diseases, ignorance of basic hygiene, bad sanitation, impure water, and poor nutrition. Epidemics of cholera carried children off in their thousands, and other waterborne diseases, such as diphtheria and enteric fever, raged in the cities. On a less stupendous scale scarlet fever, measles and whooping cough accounted for many childhood deaths. In fact at one point things were so serious that an Act of Parliament was passed in 1875 decreeing that no child under the age of five years old could be insured for more than £6.

Help came when harmful bacteria were identified and methods of immunizing against them were developed. Infectious diseases are now largely a thing of the past – hence the closing of the special fever hospitals.

What has happened in recent years, however, is that a large number of other adverse factors have entered the environment. These have led to conditions such as hyperactivity, dyslexia and other learning disabilities, and a great increase in chronic illnesses such as asthma, eczema, epilepsy and digestive disorders. Perhaps the most difficult of these conditions in the family context is hyperactivity.

The Hyperactive Child

The hyperactive child lives in a constant state of over-stimulation or, some would have it, under-inhibition. For reasons we will later investigate, his central nervous system is in a permanent state of 'go'. The hyperactive child is constantly moving – running, walking, climbing and bouncing about. He is quite unable to sit still and attempts to make him do so will result in hysterical outbursts. His activity will continue even when he is overtired and overwrought to the pitch of tears and tantrums. Even when he is exhausted he finds it hard to sleep. When he does drop off he tends to sleep lightly and restlessly, and wake early. He may often wake in the night, crying and screaming for reasons he cannot explain.

Any form of stimulation may encourage feverish excitement which will escalate into hysterical behaviour and often end in screaming and crying. He is very easily stimulated and very hard to calm down. Instructions are ignored, he cannot concentrate on a task for more than a second, and attempts to pressurize him will lead to hysterical outbursts.

The parents know that their child has a severe problem that is causing him and them endless distress, but the casual observer will probably dismiss him as a 'spoilt brat', and place the blame on him or his parents.

So far we have described the severely hyperactive child. As with all physical conditions, there are degrees of severity, from the severely afflicted child to the mildly affected. There is no magical 'cut-off' point beyond which a child is hyperactive and before which he is not hyperactive.

Symptoms of hyperactivity
Not all hyperactive children/adults will suffer every symptom listed at one and the same time – they may vary in number and intensity. From puberty onwards or earlier some children seem to improve, but from our limited knowledge of adult hyperactives there are certainly quite a number of residual problems such as insomnia, abnormal

thirst, lack of ability to concentrate.

From the Hyperactive Children's Support Group surveys it appears that many hyperactive children come from families with a history of 'allergies', hay fever, eczema, asthma, and in a large number of cases, mothers with migraine.

Hyperactive children often seem to suffer from 'colic' as small babies, sometimes with eczema, asthma, ear, nose and throat problems, rhinitis (catarrh), tummy problems, etc. This is possibly because their 'immune system' is not fully developed. (Hyperactive children are often very immature in relation to their chronological age.)

One of the symptoms which we have found in a high percentage of hyperactive children (male and female) is an *abnormal thirst*.

Group 1: Behavioural disorders

1. Constant motion
    Walks on toes
    Runs not walks
    Rocks or jiggles legs
    Cot rocking, head banging

2. Excitable, impulsive behaviour
    Unpredictable behaviour
    Panics easily
    Cries easily and often
    Whining, clinging behaviour
    Intolerance of failure and frustration
    Demands must be met immediately
    Diminished ability to experience pleasure

3. Poor sleeping habits
    Nightmares
    Has difficulty getting to sleep
    Easy to awaken
    Cries out in sleep

Fears sleep
Often abnormally thirsty

4. Short attention span
Unable to concentrate
Flits from one object to another

5. Compulsive aggression
Disruption at home and at school
Compulsive touching of everything and everyone
Disturbs other children
Molests pets
Destructive (toys, household articles, structural
    components)

6. Cannot be diverted from action, even if life-threatening
Punishment of no avail (leads to frustration or tantrum)

7. Mutilation
Scratching, biting
Picking, tearing skin

8. *In older children*
Lying
Abusive language
Stealing
Arson (occasionally)
Withdrawn
Delinquent
Fighting (conflict with peers)

Group 2: Muscle involvement

1. *Gross muscle*
Clumsy
Trips when walking
Collides with objects
Inability to play sport, cycle, swim

2. *Fine muscle*
Poor eye/hand co-ordination

Difficulty with buttoning, tying, fastening, writing, drawing (some children can draw beautifully but are still clumsy, i.e., they do not have all symptoms)
Speech difficulties – stuttering, stammering, pronunciation
Reading – dyslexia

Group 3: Clinical pattern of cognitive and perceptual disturbance

1. Auditory/memory deficits
2. Visual/memory deficits
3. Poor comprehension
4. Disturbance in optical orientation (up and down, left and right)
5. Difficulty in reasoning (simple maths problems, meaning of words)

What Causes Hyperactivity?

Many factors recently introduced into the environment appear to be contributory causes to the epidemic of hyperactivity.

Heavy metal contamination

Heavy metals, for example lead, are antagonistic to essential minerals in the body such as zinc, manganese and chromium which activate enzyme systems. From conception, the child is at risk from heavy metal contamination. For example, the lead content of the air we breathe has risen sharply, due particularly to the higher lead content of petrol and also to the increase of car ownership in post-war Britain.

Both excess lead or copper in a mother's body can affect the nervous system of a child before birth, as may cadmium from cigarette smoking, or aluminium from saucepans or food cooked in aluminium foil containers.

Factory agriculture

Factory farming has led to an alarming assortment of chemical imbalances in our food. Oversimplistic soil-boosting fertilizers, containing mainly nitrogen, phosphorous and potassium, encourage the rapid growth of plants that alters the trace mineral content. The plants grow at an unnatural rate and so do not take up as much of such trace minerals as zinc, manganese, chromium, selenium and magnesium as they would normally do. This means there is a lower level of these minerals in the foods, even normal natural foods.

Non-degradable insecticides have been designed to destroy choline in the insect's body, thus preventing it from taking up manganese (which is necessary for the function of the nervous system) and this eventually kills it. Such insecticides may have a similar cumulative effect on the human body. Manganese deficiency is frequently found in hyperactive children and children with allergies. Herbicides kill the macrobacteria in the top soil inhibiting uptake. Macrobacteria facilitate the uptake of minerals. Wheat may be induced to produce more grain per head by hormone manipulation. Then a hormone inhibitor is introduced to restrict growth of the stem, as the heavy grain will otherwise blow down in rough weather.

Antibiotics in milk and meat come from the routine doses given to cattle to prevent infectious disease. Antibiotics destroy intestinal flora (bacteria necessary for digestion) in the human gut, thus interfering with the normal breakdown and assimilation of food.

Extra hormones are given to promote rapid weight gain in animals. Chemicals may be sprayed on fruit to prevent it ripening too soon; sometimes the fruit is later dyed to look riper than it is.

All these chemicals, and those added by the food manufacturers add up to a formidable bombardment of the immature gut and central nervous systems.

Alcohol

The consumption of alcohol has risen in this country over the last twenty or thirty years, especially among young women. It is well documented that the use of alcohol in pregnancy may result in retardation with hyperactivity in the baby. The precise amount of alcohol, if any, that can be taken during pregnancy *without risk* is not yet known.

Artificial additives

Also unknown is the full effect produced by many artificial chemical colourings, flavourings, preservatives and other chemical additives. Products such as mono-sodium glutamate are added to food not to enhance it in any way, but to artificially stimulate the taste buds of the consumer. Many of these additives may be eaten together in the course of a day. The effect of such combinations has never been scientifically investigated but such additives have been found to be associated with hyperactivity in children.[1]

Drugs

It is well known that such drugs as 'tranquillizers' have the very reverse effect on a hyperactive child. What may not be so well known is that in many major cities the tap water will have been 'purified' and recycled many times. The residues of these drugs may be present in the drinking water from the urine of people who have been using them. Added to this we are told to flush unwanted medicines down the lavatory. When the water is then recycled for further use, it may not be entirely safe.

All of these pollutants, and no doubt many more we are not yet aware of, combine to have a devastating effect on the immature central nervous system of today's child.

Nutritional Deficiencies

At the same time as an ever increasing number of chemicals are being added to our daily diet, and drinking water, research shows that essential nutrients are being extracted from basic foodstuffs during processing.

For example, from what used to be known as 'the staff of life' (the ubiquitous loaf of white bread), there has been removed: 87 per cent of the chromium, 91 per cent of the manganese, 81 per cent of the iron, 70 per cent of the cobalt, between 70 per cent and 90 per cent of the copper, 83 per cent of the zinc, 50 per cent of molybdenum and 83 per cent of the magnesium that would be found in a whole wheat loaf. In addition, much of the B complex vitamins and vitamin E are removed. Of thiamin, vitamin B_1, 77 per cent is removed, 80 per cent of the riboflavin is removed, 81 per cent of the niacin, 71 per cent of the pyridoxine, 50 per cent of the pantothenic acid, 67 per cent of the folic acid and 86 per cent of the vitamin E. All of these nutrients are essential for the digestion of wheat and so as we eat the white bread, they are leeched from our body's reserves.

The Effects of Living With a Hyperactive Child

Unchecked and untreated, environmental poisons and dietary deficiencies can play such havoc with the nervous system of a tiny child that these children can, from babyhood, be exhibiting atypical behaviour which in an older person would be recognized as a severe degree of mental illness. To live all day with someone who may be unable to keep still, unable to sleep, unable to respond to affection, who is subject to uncontrollable tantrums, who may constantly expose themselves and others to danger, who is unable to learn even simple tasks, and who does not respond to the spoken word, is something of an emotional marathon!

All parents (especially mothers) of hyperactive children are under an almost intolerable degree of stress that is seldom understood by the outsider. In many cases it may drive the mother to seek help from tranquillizers for herself, but in some mothers tranquillizers release inhibitions in her stressed nervous system, so that she may batter the child.[2] The HACSG therefore recommend very strongly that mothers under stress avoid these drugs which often worsen rather than improve the whole situation.

The Hyperactive Children's Support Group (HACSG)

The Hyperactive Children's Support Group was founded in 1977 by Mrs Sally Bunday and her mother Mrs Irene Colquhoun. It was the direct result of Sally's experiences with her own hyperactive son, her frustration at not being able to find understanding and help from the medical profession, and her feeling that not enough was being done for these children and their parents. (See Appendix 2, p.117.)

The aims of the group are to:

1. help and support hyperactive children and their parents (not financially);

2. encourage the formation of local groups or contacts where parents may get together for mutual support and understanding;

3. urge the medical profession, health and education authorities to take more interest in the day-to-day problems of hyperactive children and adolescents;

4. promote urgent research into causes of hyperactivity; whether it be linked to chemical food additives, nutritional deficiencies, food allergies and/or environmental pollution;

5. press for early and proper diagnosis of hyperactivity, possible treatments and management, and to disseminate information to all interested parties.

Why is a self-help group needed?

This is an important question. If such a condition as hyperactivity exists, why is it not recognized by the medical profession and subjected to scientific investigation? And why is help not available through the accepted channels? In our experience it is for the following reasons.

Recent changes in the amounts of chemical pollutants and poisons which enter our bodies, and the sharp reduction in intake of the nutrients needed to maintain growth, development and health, have led to a bewildering spectrum of effects on the human body. As the brain, central nervous system and endocrine system are part of the body, many of these changes manifest as severe problems with mental development and behaviour. Just as the more serious effects of physical disease are commonly seen in the very young or the very old, so we are finding the more disastrous effects of this manipulation showing in the very young as hyperactivity, learning difficulties, allergic syndromes or chronic illness. With the very old, senility and confused thought are becoming an increasing problem.

The parents of the hyperactive child are therefore facing problems of which neither they, their parents, nor their GPs have had much previous experience. So there is virtually no one to whom they can turn for advice.

Most GPs have had no training in environmental hazards and their subsequent repercussions. They have no choice therefore but to prescribe drugs or to recommend psychoanalysis.

In the past drugs have proved neither effective nor completely free from harmful side-effects.

With psychoanalysis the situation is even more confused. A common result of misapplied and misunderstood psychoanalytic theories is that parents seeking help with a problem child are often subjected to indifference, implied blame and rudeness. Indeed it appears that research into biochemical causes of hyperactivity and other mental illnesses has been severely inhibited and hampered by these attitudes.

This, briefly, is why lay organizations have had to step into the gap. We are hoping these attitudes will change as medical practitioners become more interested in environmental causes of hyperactivity and see the results of the HACSG's approach.

In the meantime the HACSG continues to gather information. In this book we have brought together all that we know so far about methods of treatment which many hundreds of parents have tried and found to be invaluable.

The added bonus of the approaches we suggest is that they very often bring improved health to the whole family.

Notes

[1] This has been documented by Dr Ben Feingold of California. Dr Feingold hypothesized that familiar and beneficial minerals such as zinc and manganese might be used by the body to 'coat' foreign substances to ensure them a safe passage through the kidneys or liver.

[2] It was recorded in a letter in the *British Medical Journal* (1 February 1975, p.26) that 92 per cent of mothers who battered their babies were on tranquillizers. The letter was in response to an article which appeared in the issue of 18 January 1975 on the side-effects of commonly used tranquillizers.

1

THE SELF-HELP PROGRAMME

The HACSG has studied a great deal of background work on hyperactivity, learning difficulties and disturbed mental development, and the therapies developed to offset the problems.[1] From what we know at present we believe that parents should look for and correct the following factors in the hyperactive child.

1. *Nutritional deficiencies, particularly vitamins of the B complex, A, C, D, and E, calcium, magnesium, manganese, zinc, chromium, selenium, cobalt and essential fatty acids*
These nutrients are to be found abundantly in fresh wholefoods, especially in dairy products, fish, meat, poultry, and offal, salads and fruits eaten raw, wholegrains, nuts, pulses and sprouted seeds. They are *noticeably deficient* from many convenience foods. (See Chapter 2 for diet suggestions.)

Of the first seventy mothers who replied to a questionnaire sent out by the HACSG, sixty-eight had found significant improvement in the child from following this régime alone. Sleeping problems improved and hyperactivity was very significantly reduced. For some children (particularly those who live in a comparatively unpolluted area) following a diet of fresh wholefoods entirely free from artificial additives, and eliminating certain obvious factors from the environment (e.g. aluminium saucepans), is sufficient for the child to improve. Other children need further investigation.

2. *Sensitivities to food allergens, to pollutants and coeliac disease*
The withdrawal of certain foods and/or external factors
which affect the child adversely can also bring an improvement. (We will discuss this further in Chapter 3.)

3. *Heavy metal toxicities and severe trace mineral deficiencies*
Many children suffering from hyperactivity have been
found to have a high body level of toxic metals. Often this
is lead or aluminium, more rarely it is mercury, cadmium
and/or over-high copper or selenium. High levels can be
detected by hair analysis and then reduced by specific
diets, a cleansing programme and by supplementation of
vitamin C and trace minerals. The same analysis will
reveal trace mineral deficiencies – these can be replenished
by supplementation. (Further details are given in Chapter
4.)

4. *Facial defects and skull deformities, including the high raised
palate*
Many hyperactive children have long, narrow 'pinched'-
looking faces, with pointed chins, overcrowded teeth,
and low-set protruding ears. The top teeth may be pushed
forward and the chin may recede.[2]

Many hyperactive children (possibly because they were
short of essential nutrients in the womb) may also have
somewhat poorly formed asymmetrical skulls and high
raised palates. This type of aberrant skull formation may
inhibit the flow of blood and cerebro-spinal fluid to the
brain cells and thus impair the supply of oxygen, blood
sugar and other nutrients. A high raised palate may put
pressure on the base of the brain.

A controlled study by Mr Colin Dove, of the British
School of Osteopathy has recently been carried out in
collaboration with a consultant psychiatrist, with a large
number of retarded children in an NHS hospital. Mr
Dove and the psychiatrist in charge found that a programme
of cranial osteopathy helped children with high raised

palates, and/or malformed skulls.

5. *Adverse reaction to fluorescent lighting*

The work of John Ott[3] suggests that fluorescent lights, and in some cases the rays from the television tube, may have an adverse effect on the central nervous system of hyperactive children. This needs further investigation but the possibility is one more thing to be borne in mind by parents who are trying to help their child. If he seems to react unfavourably to fluorescent lighting, try to rely on daylight or other forms of artificial light as much as possible, and avoid exposing him to a fluorescent bulb for long periods of time.

Television viewing should also be kept within limits. During the summer months the child should be encouraged to play outside as much as possible. (As research progresses the HACSG hopes to give more information on this particular subject.)

The self-help programme

The programme we would initially suggest is the diet given in Chapter 2. This diet consists of fresh wholefoods and excludes all artificial additives, flavourings, colourings, etc. We suggest that the child follows this diet for eight weeks, using *Junomac* and *Junoiron* supplements during this initial period to combat long-standing deficiencies.

At first the child may have a poor appetite and may not take well to the natural diet if he is used to a lot of very sugary foods. A supplement (e.g. *Junomac*) that increases the amount of vitamin B, zinc and manganese and other nutrients will help increase the appetite and in turn may also help him to accept his new foods better.

Evaluate the child's progress. For some children diet alone will bring enormous improvement; with about half the children, however, there will still be a lot to be done.

If you have seen little or no improvement at the end of the initial eight weeks it may also be necessary to search out foods or other types of allergens, and to obtain a hair analysis to see if the child has a mineral imbalance. He may either have a high body level of toxic metal (such as lead) or he may be severely deficient in essential minerals. It may then be necessary to start a cleansing programme and give more specific mineral supplements (see Chapter 4).

With children who do not respond to the diet, it is also worth looking carefully at the shape of the head and comparing the palate shape with that of other children. The hyperactive child's palate may seem to go right up like a church roof inside his mouth! If you feel that his skull is malformed in this way and that cranial osteopathy would help, seek expert assistance.[4]

Notes

[1] Much of the practical work has been done by Dr Ben Feingold and Dr Elizabeth Lodge Rees of California, Dr Abram Hoffer and Dr Glyn Green of Canada, Dr U. Blackwood of Ohio, and the late Dr Weston Price of California. Helpful dietary advice has been found in the papers of the McCarrison Society, The Henry Doubleday Association and The Soil Association.

We have also been helped in our work by the books of Dr Richard Mackarness, Dr Carl Pfeiffer and Dr Henry Schroeder, and many others writing on allergy and diet.

Animal studies that we have found helpful have included the work of Dr Bert Varlee of Harvard University Medical School, Drs Oberleas and Caldwell of Wayne State University, Michigan, and Dr Lucille Hurley of the University of California.

[2] These features have been clearly described and photographed by Dr Weston Price in *Nutrition and Physical Degeneration*, his book about the effects of a refined diet on children's bone structure. He ascribes ill-formed bone structure to the low level of calcium and fat soluble vitamins in our Western diet. His research was limited as techniques for measuring trace minerals were not available to him in the 1930s.

[3] See John Ott's *Health and Light* New York: Pocket Books.

[4] A list of qualified osteopaths can be obtained from Dr Colin Dove, British School of Osteopathy, 16 Buckingham Palace Road, London SW1.

The above scientific papers can be obtained from the Foresight Library. Write to Mrs Jill Clarke, 8 Duchess Close, Strood, Rochester, Kent.

2
NUTRITION

In this chapter we want first to take a general look at food and then discuss in detail vitamins and minerals. The rest of the chapter sets out general principles for planning meals, followed by detailed menu suggestions and recipes.

We have found that many hundreds of hyperactive children respond very favourably to a varied wholefood diet entirely free from chemical additives. The diet recommended eliminates excess sugar (extra sugar means extra hyperactivity). Food is only sweetened when absolutely necessary and then with raw Barbados sugar or Muscavado sugar, honey or molasses, used very sparingly. It is a good idea to vary the diet as much as possible and not rely too heavily on wheat and milk products as these are very common allergens in the hyperactive child.

For simplicity we have divided food into four main groups – cereals, vegetables and fruit, meat, dairy products – and will look at 'good foods' and 'foods to be avoided' within each category. (See also 'Safe Food' list published by HACSG, and Foodwatch. Details in Useful Addresses.)

CEREALS

Good foods
Wholewheat bread, i.e., bread containing 100 per cent of the grain. Some bread is merely refined flour coloured with gravy browning. Check with your baker and don't accept anything less!

Wholewheat rolls, scones, cakes.

Wholewheat cereals, e.g. *Shredded Wheat, Shreddies, Wholewheat Force, Puffed Wheat, Sunnybisk,* and all natural muesli cereals (beware of those with added sugar).

Porridge – made from pinhead oatmeal, millet, wholewheat meal, pot barley, maize meal.

Wholegrain crispbreads, e.g. *Ryvita, Vitawheat*.

Wholewheat biscuits, oatcakes etc. (Biscuits can be made at home using wholewheat flour or oats with raw sugar or molasses, see p.59.)

Flour – whole maize (polenta), yellow and green split pea, potato, rice. Almost any white flour recipe can be adapted to suit these ingredients.

Pastry – 'brown' pastry is difficult to handle; compromise with ⅔ wholewheat to ⅓ refined flour. (81-85 per cent stoneground flours are also available.)

Tapioca, sago, wholewheat semolina, wholewheat pasta.

Foods to be avoided
White flour and all white flour products, e.g. cakes, biscuits, pastries, cake mixes, pudding mixes.

White bread.

VEGETABLES

Good foods
Raw vegetables and salads[1]
All fresh vegetables can safely be eaten raw except potatoes and some pulses. It is a good idea for a child to have a raw salad every day. Salads can contain any of the following, whole, chopped or grated: lettuce, endive, chicory, white or red cabbage, cress, cauliflower, radishes,

tomato*, cucumber*, celery, onions, carrots, button mushrooms, Chinese leaves, watercress, small peas, sweet peppers*, and all sprouted seeds like alfalfa and mung beans.

For flavour add all types of fruit*, dried fruit*, nuts, seeds, and fresh herbs.

Salad dressing can be made with sunflower seed oil, honey and a few drops of cider* or tarragon vinegar. Home-made mayonnaise, yoghurt or soured cream can also be used.

Avocado pears are particularly rich in vitamin E, and all leaf vegetables are good sources of linoleic acid, an important essential fatty acid. Both these nutrients assist the take-up of trace minerals and are very important to the hyperactive child.

Cooking vegetables
Where cooking is necessary, the following guidelines will help preserve vitamins and minerals.

1. Vegetables should be picked as short a time as possible before the meal (if home-grown) and then washed quickly and cooked immediately.

2. Where possible vegetables should always be scrubbed with a soft brush rather than peeled or scraped.

3. Cook vegetables in as little water as possible.

4. Use the cooking water for gravy, soups, or stews, as it contains a lot of goodness.

5. Invest in a 'steamer'. All vegetables taste better if they are steamed rather than boiled.

*Throughout the book we use this symbol to identify salicylate-containing foods. These should be avoided by any salicylate-sensitive child.

6. Keep cut surfaces to a minimum, so that vitamins/minerals are not leached out.

Potatoes are best baked or steamed. Other vegetables can be stir-fried in a little sunflower seed oil (or similar) and the oil served with the vegetables.

Pieces of bean sprouts, celery, carrot, nuts, sunflower seeds, fresh or dried fruit, etc. can be used instead of sweets. Vegetable and natural fruit juices can be used in place of squashes. (*St Ivel/Farmer's Wife* juices are sugar and colourant free.)

FRUITS

A number of hyperactive children react badly to the salicylate-containing fruits. Omit all fruits listed below. After a good response to the diet (say eight weeks) introduce them *one at a time* and if there is no poor response, add them gradually, introducing them occasionally and not too much at any one time.

*Salicylate-containing fruits**: almonds, apples, apricots, peaches, plums, prunes, oranges, tomatoes, tangerines, cucumber, blackberries, strawberries, raspberries, gooseberries, cherries, currants, grapes, raisins.

Good foods
All other fruits, dried, fresh or stewed.

Home-bottled fruit (bottled in water only).

Home-pressed juices.

Cooking fruit
Fruit is best stewed in a glass dish in the oven or in an enamel saucepan. If necessary use a little raw sugar, honey or molasses.

Foods to be avoided

Fruits tinned in heavy syrup, which has a lot of extra sugar, may have lead from the seams of the tins, and in some cases artificial colouring. Raw potatoes or potatoes that have turned green with frost – these contain nitrite which is a poison.

Tinned vegetables, which will have lost all vestige of vitamin C.

Commercially-frozen peas and beans may be treated with EDTA before freezing, which removes trace minerals.

Vegetables cooked the day before and reheated – the vitamin C content will be nil.

MEAT

Good foods

Fresh meat, bacon, ham (ask your butcher if these contain nitrates and other artificial preservatives – if they do, avoid them), liver, heart, kidney, brains, sweetbreads, tongues, game, most poultry, deep-sea fish, and fish roes.

Fresh sausages free from preservatives – a local butcher may supply these, but check that they are preservative-free.

Pâté – made at home from fish, lamb's liver, or free-range poultry liver.

Meat from organic farms is best but may be hard to find although it is getting easier all the time, enquire locally, or see the 'Useful Addresses' section at the end of this book or apply to the Foresight Association. (The Wholefood Shop, 24 Paddington Street, London W1 supplies it.)[2]

Meat should be bought as fresh as possible; venison, rabbit, game bird, pigeon and quail and all sea foods are the best meats nowadays as the animals have not been intensively farmed. Mutton, lamb and offal from sheep is less intensively farmed than beef, pig products and chicken. The latter may have been subjected to artificial fattening and/or extra copper in feed processes and hormones to stimulate weight gain etc. They should, therefore, be used more sparingly.

Cooking meat
Meat is best spit-roasted, grilled or stewed with vegetables and pulses, preferably in bone stock. The stock will then contain many of the minerals and should not be thrown away, but can be eaten with a spoon or used later for soup. Bone broth made from simmering joint bones, poultry carcasses, etc. is valuable for calcium and makes delicious gravy or soup.

Foods to be avoided
Stale meat and meat fried in stale fat.

Twice-cooked meat.

Tinned meats which contain sodium nitrate.
Commercial pâtés, packet bacon, ham, sausages and pies which contain preservatives and sometimes monosodium glutamate. (Some tinned sauces for meat contain monosodium glutamate and preservatives[2].)

Ready-cooked frozen meats and fish coated with dyed breadcrumbs, batter, etc.

Capons and intensively-reared turkeys who may have been given extra hormones to promote unnaturally fast weight gain.

DAIRY PRODUCTS

Many children react badly to cow's milk and its products these days, possibly because the promotion of bottle-feeding has led to earlier and earlier weaning on to a sugar and cow's milk formula with resulting adverse reactions. Some babies are still fed with cow's milk in the first few days of life in hospital. This section is for the more fortunate to whom cow's milk is a good friend. Egg white may also cause allergic reaction – in some cases eczema and asthma.

Good foods

Free-range eggs – they have more flavour and harder shells. The membrane surrounding the yolk does not break so easily when you try to fry or separate them. This all indicates a hen has been allowed to pick and peck all day long at will and has taken in a better diet with more trace mineral content than that of the pathetic prisoner in the battery. Fresh eggs keep for a couple of weeks, so it is worth making a journey to get them.

Unpasteurized cream.

Fresh milk – not homogenized.

Cheeses, *except* those which contain preservatives or colouring (as some processed cheeses do).

Butter, *except* those containing artificial colourants (see p.55).

Goat's milk, cheese and yoghurt. The fat in goat's milk is much nearer to human milk fats than the fat in cow's milk. The milk can be served as milkshakes made with bananas, honey, peanut butter, etc., or pulped fruit.*

Junket – made the old-fashioned way with rennet.

Ice-cream – made at home with unpasteurized cream or goat's milk, eggs and honey; with or without fruit pulp for flavouring depending on whether the child is salicylate-sensitive or not.

Fruit soufflés, syllabubs, fruit* 'snows' made with whipped white of egg.

There are, of course, no end to egg dishes and the changes can be rung with eggs from ducks, geese and guinea fowl – all of which are less likely to be intensively farmed. Quail eggs, in season, are delicious and recent research suggests that they may be useful in combatting certain types of allergy.

Foods to be avoided
Tinned evaporated milk from tins with lead seams.

Dried milks, as exposure to light and/or drying destroys lysine, arachidonic acid and some of the B complex vitamins, all of which are important to the hyperactive child.

VITAMINS

Each vitamin has a different role to play in nourishing the body. Vitamins are divided into two types, the fat-soluble ones – A, D, E and K – and the water-soluble ones – C and the many Bs. The fat-soluble vitamins can be stored in the body in quite large amounts. The water-soluble vitamins are most vulnerable. They cannot be stored to any great extent and therefore need to be replenished daily.

Vitamin A
Role: good for the eyes, the internal membranes. It is needed for normal growth and contributes to a healthy skin, hair and nails.
Found in animal tissues which contain pre-formed vitamins, dairy produce (milk, butter, cheese), egg yolk, liver, kidneys, sweetbreads, fatty fish and fish-liver oils. Man can also synthesize this vitamin from carotene which is found in leafy vegetables such as chard, kale, spinach, broccoli, string beans, carrots, tomatoes, marrow, red peppers, apricots, peaches and sweet potato.
Destroyed by strong light, heat, long, slow cooking, de-

hydration. Wilted vegetables lose a high percentage of carotene. Liquid paraffin prevents its absorption and should be avoided.

Vitamin B group

At least five of this group are needed to break down glucose and produce energy. They are needed for the metabolism of carbohydrates (sugars and starches), fats and proteins and to maintain the central nervous system. Deficiency in adults can cause depression, inability to concentrate, insomnia, 'mania' and other forms of mental breakdown. *The B complex vitamins are particularly vital to the hyperactive child as one of their main functions is to regulate the central nervous system.*

Separate vitamins improve muscle tone, regulate digestion, guard against constipation, utilize sugar, militate against allergy and perform many other vital functions in the body. One vitamin, nicotinamide, alone performs forty-two separate functions! Lack of the B vitamins can lead to complete physical and mental breakdown, but they are all removed from commonly used modern foodstuffs by the refining process.

B_1 thiamine

Found in brewer's yeast, wheat germ, whole grains, whole cereals, nuts, peanut butter, dried peas, beans, soya beans, lentils, pork, ham, kidney, heart, liver and eggs.
Destroyed by cooking and storage in a warm place. It is quickly lost in an alkaline medium.

B_2 riboflavin

Found in brewer's yeast, milk, butter, yoghurt, cheese, eggs, whole grains, wheat germ, soya beans, peas, lentils, cooked leafy vegetables and lean meat and liver.
Destroyed by light.

B_3 (in USA) nicotinamide
Found in brewer's yeast, wheat germ, whole grains, nuts, peanuts, eggs, green vegetables, fish, lean meats, liver, kidneys, potato.

B_5 (in USA) pantothenic acid
Folic acid and biotin are needed for absorption.
Found in brewer's yeast, wheat germ, whole grains, bran, green vegetables, liver, kidney and heart.

B_6 pyridoxine
Found in brewer's yeast, wheat germ, bran, molasses, liver, heart, kidney, peanuts and mushrooms and just under the skin of potatoes (peeling potatoes may totally remove it).

B_{12} cynocobalamin
Found in milk, cheese, eggs, fish, most lean meats, liver and kidney. Vegetarians are more likely to be lacking in this vitamin. Vegans must use supplements.

Folic acid
Found in milk, nuts, all green vegetables, brewer's yeast, liver, kidneys.
Destroyed by cooking.

Inositol
Found in brewer's yeast, wheat germ, whole grains, oatmeal, corn, molasses and liver.

Choline
Needs pantothenate (B_5) for absorption.
Found in wheat germ, egg yolk, brewer's yeast, green vegetables, legumes, lean meat, brains, liver, kidneys.
Destroyed by an alkaline medium.

Biotin
Found in brewer's yeast, milk, eggs, mushrooms, liver and kidneys.

In practice most B vitamins are found together and eating whole grain foods, with possibly the addition of brewer's yeast, either in gravies, soups and stews in powdered form, or as tablets, should ensure a steady supply. Eggs, green vegetables and offal are particularly rich sources, as is toasted wheat germ, which can be sprinkled on cereals or salads.

   Antibiotic therapy affects the supply of these vitamins because the drugs kill the normal intestinal bacteria which help us to digest food. One of the reasons why hyperactive children so often react to milk may be that the level of antibiotics in the milk could be interfering with the absorption of vitamin B. A deficiency of several of the B group of vitamins leads to skin problems. This *may* account for the fact that when children with eczema come off milk many of them improve.

Vitamin C
Role: necessary for the functioning of collagen – a substance which holds the cells together. It is very important therefore for healthy tissues, blood vessels, bones, teeth and gums. It also helps combat fatigue, counteract infections, remove toxins from the body. It also helps the absorption of iron.
Found in citrus fruits*, guavas, peppers*, pimentos, rose-hips*, tomatoes*, cabbage, fresh strawberries*, salad greens, Brussels sprouts, broccoli, apples*, bananas, lettuce, potatoes, peas, blackcurrants*, sweet corn, melon and grapes*.
Destroyed by storing, soaking and boiling. Frozen foods lose vitamin C after they have thawed for an hour. Cooking once and later re-heating destroys it completely.

Vitamin D

Role: assists the uptake of magnesium and calcium, so contributing to the growth and solidity of bones and teeth.
Found in dairy produce – butter, cream, milk, fatty fish, eggs, fish-liver oils. *If* the natural oils of the body are on the skin (i.e., not following bathing), vitamin D can be made by the body in conjunction with sunlight. Cow's milk has about half the vitamin D content of human milk.
Destroyed by liquid paraffin which prevents its absorption.

Vitamin E

Role: necessary for maintaining suppleness and toughness of all skins, linings of the body, and muscle tone.
Found in wheat germ oil, whole wheat, milk, egg yolk, unrefined vegetable oils, green vegetables, especially lettuce and avocado pears.
Destroyed by rancidity in fats.

Vitamin K

Role: essential for clotting of the blood.
Found in cauliflower, spinach, kale, alfalfa, soya bean oil, and pig's liver.

Bioflavonoids

Role: thought to assist in maintaining blood vessel walls.
Found in citrus fruits*, grapes*, blackcurrants*, and rosehips*.

MINERALS

The body needs minerals for numerous functions. Hair analysis of hyperactive children has shown that they have a short supply of most minerals – in particular magnesium, zinc, manganese and chromium. When the lacking vitamins and minerals are adequately supplemented, many hyperactive children improve enormously.

Calcium
Adequate intake is important from birth to death.
Role: essential for bone growth and calcification of the infant cartilages and teeth; for heart muscle function, for contraction of all muscles, for the substance holding body cells together, and correct function of some cell membranes.
Found in milk and cheese. Where these are not tolerated Dolomite tablets should be taken daily. Also in apples, bananas, oranges, green vegetables, eggs, potatoes and carrots, bone broth or jelly, whole grain products, fatty fish – herrings, sardines, salmon.
Deficiency can cause pain in the joints, brittle bones and poor teeth.

Elderly arthritic adults who have eaten white bread (which has chalk instead of calcium) for decades, improve spontaneously over about a year when they change to whole cereals. Chalk may not be an acceptable substitute to all bodies!

Magnesium
Role: helps transmit nerve impulses to muscles. Is necessary for the growth and repair of body cells. It has been found to help children to become calmer and more responsive to the spoken word. It is a vital component in numerous biochemical reactions.
Found in nuts, soya beans, green vegetables, whole grains. Vegetable water from cooking should be kept and consumed.
Deficiencies can inhibit brain development, increase vulnerability to infections and can cause muscle twitches, cramps, tremor and emotional irritability.

Iron
Role: essential for the oxygen-carrying constituent of blood.
Found in brewer's yeast, wheat germ, whole grains, egg

yolks, fish, red meat, liver, raisins and all dried fruit, green vegetables.

Vitamin C is necessary for complete uptake of iron in food. For children who are not salicylate-sensitive, apples are helpful (they contain malic acid which helps iron absorption) and/or raisins soaked for twelve hours in lemon juice.

Iron cooking pans may contribute trace amounts.

Copper
Role: necessary for the efficient absorption of iron from food and for brain development and function. Since the invention of copper water-pipes, deficiency is less frequent. Needed in minute quantities and generally sufficient is absorbed from food or water. However, often found to be at very low levels in hair of autistic or retarded children. This may sometimes be due to prolonged use of medication to control epilepsy, and is worthy of further investigation.

Manganese
Role: essential for growth and skeletal development. Carries oxygen to the nucleus of the cell and is essential for correct brain function. This includes thought, memory and concentration. Frequently found to be *very low* in the hair of hyperactive children and epileptics. Both conditions respond to supplementation (see p.44). Choline, pantothenic acid, folic acid, biotin, vitamin B_6, essential fatty acids, and vitamin E are required for absorption/usage. *Cantassium* make a supplement *Mangamac* to combine these nutrients in one preparation.
Found in nuts, whole grains, dried fruits, green vegetables, seeds, bran, brown rice, oats, buckwheat, onions, strawberries*, bananas, apples*, pineapples, green beans, liver, snails(!), poultry and seafoods.

Chromium
Role: needed for insulin to utilize glucose.

Found in brewer's yeast, whole wheat, liver, beef, beets, beet sugar, molasses and mushrooms.
Deficiencies found in 'reactive hypoglycaemia' and diabetes.

Zinc
Role: needed for cell multiplication, i.e., mental and physical development. Found to be especially important in pregnancy, puberty, teething and when fighting infection. Essential too for healthy growth, skin, wound healing, hair growth.
Found in all raw vegetables, especially peas and carrots, green vegetables, nuts, a small quantity in all fruit, liver, lean meat, chicken, whole grains, wheat buds, bran, oatmeal, eggs, milk, North Sea herrings and oysters.

Selenium
Role: essential for the skin and the pancreas. Important in the prevention of cancer.
Found in brewer's yeast, garlic, liver, eggs, brown rice, wholewheat bread. It is not included in the Juno supplements as raised levels can be found following the use of shampoos containing selenium.

SUPPLEMENTS

Junomac and *Junoiron* are supplements which can be given to children who need help to make up vitamin and mineral deficiencies more quickly. They are available from health food stores without a prescription.

For young children the tablets can be crushed and mixed in with food.

Junomac formula
Vitamin A   200iu
Vitamin D   25iu
Vitamin E   30iu
Evening primrose oil   30iu

Ascorbic acid (vitamin C)   50 mg
Vitamin B   2 mg
Nicotinamide   35 mg
Pantothenic acid   7.5 mg
B_6 6 mg
B_{12} 2 mcg
Folic acid   10 mcg
PABA   15 mg
Pangamate   2.5 mg
Choline   65 mg
Inositol   50 mg
Biotin   1 mcg
Zinc   0.2 mg
Manganese   0.2 mg
Chromium   1.8 mg
Calcium   8.6 mg
Magnesium   5.2 mg

Junoiron formula
Calcium phosphate (mineral, trace)
Vitamin C   50 mg
Sago flour
B_{13} iron   15 mg (supplying 2 mg of iron)
Dolomite, vegetable fatty acid, natural vegetable gum
B_{13} copper   132.3 mcg (supplying 20.5 mcg of copper)

Mangamac formula
Calcium phosphate (mineral, trace)
Soya lecithin   80 mg
Evening primrose oil   66 mg
Vitamin E   66 iu
Manganese orotate   50 mg (supplying 6.5 mg of manganese)
Potato starch
Calcium pantothenate   15 mg
Vegetable fatty acid (trace)
B_6 3 mg

Natural vegetable gum
Biotin   5 mcg
Folic acid   10 mcg

Evening primrose oil

The brain and central nervous system are formed very largely of certain types of fat. These fats are found in abundance in human breast-milk, but are much less readily available from the feeding formula that is usually given as a substitute.

Essential fatty acids cannot be made by the body and must be acquired through food. The polyunsatrate of overwhelming importance in the human diet is linoleic acid – this is a major constituent of such vegetable oils as corn oil, sunflower and safflower oils.

It has been postulated that children who were deprived of breast milk from an early age may benefit from supplements of linoleic acid, and many parents have found children improve when using these vegetable oils, and in some cases goat's milk. However, linoleic acid has little biological activity, and in order to be of use to the body it must be metabolized (or converted) to gamma-linolenic acid (GLA). Studies suggest that a number of hyperactive and allergic children may be unable to metabolize essential fatty acids because they lack sufficient linoleic acid, or the necessary co-factors (zinc, B vitamins and vitamin C).

Evening primrose oil is the only substance other than human breast milk which contains the vital gamma linolenic acid. Recently evening primrose oil has been made available to the public under such brand names as *Cantassium F-500, Efamol and Naudicelle*.

The HACSG has found that supplements of zinc and other important co-factors such as vitamin B_6, nicotinamide and vitamin C, plus evening primrose oil are beneficial to hyperactive and allergic children, especially those suffering from abnormal thirst and children from 'atopic' families.

(Atopic families are those in which eczema, asthma, hayfever and allergies are common.) It would seem likely that children who were not breast-fed may need this type of fat for a period of time to replenish cells that may have been deprived in the first nine months of life.

It is not yet known whether evening primrose oil is more helpful to the children than goat's milk or safflower oil. These may suffice, so long as the child has the B vitamins, vitamin C and E, and zinc which are necessary to help metabolize linoleic acid to gamma-linolenic acid.

The suggested dosage is one capsule per two stone in body weight per day, up to a maximum of four capsules daily. Some children may benefit more from the oil being massaged into the soft skin areas, such as the stomach and inner thighs.

A reasonable amount of evening primrose oil is incorporated in *Junomac*. In some cases the child may need a larger dose, in which instance *F-500* capsules or *Efamol* may be given daily for as long as necessary. These families may also have trace mineral problems. It is vital that these be investigated. (See p.78.)

Warning: If the child is epileptic do not give evening primrose oil, first consult HACSG or Foresight for further advice.

MEALS

It is, of course, up to the individual family what foods are eaten at what times of day, as this is partly a matter of convenience and individual preference, but a child going off to school without a good breakfast will find it more difficult to sit still and concentrate and learn.

Breakfast

The hyperactive child who has not been used to eating breakfast may at first not be very hungry in the morning. (This is mainly due to the lack of the B complex vitamins, zinc and vitamins C and E, and will soon improve if he is given supplements.) In the meantime it may only be possible to get him to drink. If he is not sensitive to cow's milk or goat's milk, try a milkshake. A banana milkshake with egg and honey makes a good sustaining breakfast. If he is not salicylate-sensitive, try fruit milkshake with stewed fruit.

Later on you can try him on a little wholegrain cereal, muesli or porridge, or a cooked breakfast (bacon and egg, or fish) and some raw fruit or fruit juice. (See pp.51-53 for other suggestions.)

Try to avoid wheat cereal and wheat bread or toast at the same meal as it is important not to overload his system with wheat or dairy products to the exclusion of other foods. Raw fruit or vegetable at every meal is a good rule.

Lunch
School lunches vary enormously. Ask what the children have for lunch. If you are trying to avoid food additives, you may need to explain this. The more parents who say that their child should be kept on additive-free foods, the more the schools will get used to accommodating them. If the response is unsympathetic, ask if he can take a packed lunch.

Wholewheat sandwiches – cheese, marmite, hard-boiled egg – salads and nuts can be transported without difficulty, as can wholewheat cakes, biscuits and raw fruit. *Do not* make fish or meat sandwiches, as these can 'go off' in a warm building and cause serious illness.

The evening meal
This might be meat, fish or poultry with salad, or soup, followed by pudding.

Soup
Almost anything can go into soup, including a teaspoon of brewer's yeast, which will help increase the B vitamins.

Salads
As many raw ingredients as possible, e.g. sprouted seeds, raw mushrooms, raw cauliflower, shredded cabbage with nuts and grated carrot, mustard and cress, beetroot, celery.

Salad dressings
Oil, honey and lemon juice*, yoghurt, soured cream, French dressing, mayonnaise.

Cakes and biscuits
These are far more nutritious when made with whole-wheat flour. They can be made to rise by adding small quantities of bicarbonate of soda and cream of tartar, and by beating egg whites stiffly and folding them into the mixture (baking powder often contains additives – check the label).

Bread
You can make your own wholewheat bread, although in many areas you can buy good wholewheat bread.

Puddings
Crumbles, sponges, steamed puddings all taste better made with wholewheat flour. Stewed fruit* and milk puddings – junket, custard, ice cream, milk jelly, rice, barley, sago, tapioca – can all be used to reduce the wheat content of the diet.

The evening meal should not contain too much wheat. Salad, soup (thickened with potato or yellow or green pea flour) and certain puddings can reduce the wheat content of the diet. So too can using a variety of flours (see p.31). The aim should be to provide a wide variety of cereals and starches.

Ideas for meals
The following pages set out specific menus for ten days

which are based on the whole food, additive-free principles
we discussed earlier. They give a good picture of a
balanced diet, avoiding repetitious use of wheat – even
wholewheat! – every day. If he has a wheat cereal for
breakfast, he has a different cereal for pudding – rice, for
example, or sago – and has *Ryvita* for tea.

If he has egg, he only has it once in the day – preferably
not more than 4-5 a week.

Jam is used sparingly – perhaps once in 4 days. Salads
and raw fruit are used often if the child is not salicylate-
sensitive.

Vegetables are rotated – leaf (cabbage, lettuce, Brussels
sprouts etc.), root (turnip, carrot, parsnip, beetroot),
flower (cauliflower, broccoli, calibrese), bulb (onions
and leeks), fruit (cucumbers, marrow, pumpkin, courgette)
and mushrooms.

Meats too, rotate – brown meat (beef, lamb, pork),
white meat (poultry, rabbit), offal (heart, liver, kidneys,
brain). Fish.

All types of cereal are brought into play – as well as
wheat, rye (*Ryvita*), oats (pinhead and plain oatmeal),
rice (brown, whole, ground and flaked and rice flour),
polenta, barley (pearl barley), millet, buckwheat, sago,
tapioca, pea-flour. This makes it very easy to ring the
changes.

Potato once a day is enough. If he has rice for lunch, he
can have baked potato or mash for supper.

Ideally, the more fruit and vegetables that can be
home-grown the better. These can be completely fresh
and free from contamination.

However, 'Pick-it-Yourself' and other organic market
gardens and farms are now much more common and most
countries have several.

The Foresight Association Branch Secretaries all keep
a file of organic suppliers in their districts. In many cases
farms can supply not only fruit and vegetables, but also
wheat, meat and milk. One Foresight doctor has found

that out of six 'wheat allergic' patients, four can eat organically grown wheat without reaction. It makes practical good sense to give the organic movement in this country all the support we can.

If you do not know of a local supplier, write, enclosing a S.A.E. to Foresight, marking the envelope 'Organic Produce Supplier'.

It can get to be *fun* planning a week's menu, balancing starch, protein and fruit and vegetable – getting in a raw fruit or vegetable every day, juggling with the cereals, the types of vegetables and the types of meat.

Try to avoid all white flour and refined sugar. Excess sugar, cakes, biscuits, sweets, chocolate, etc. can result in an increase in behavioural problems and can produce excessive thirst.

It is quite an intelligence test – I am sure you can pick holes in my menu – but you get the general idea!

Shop for small amounts of food, so there are not a lot of left-overs.

Of course, children have individual allergies and individual tastes and these must be accommodated – this is just a guide, not a set of rules!

Day 1
Oatmeal porridge
Poached egg on
wholewheat toast
Fruit juice

Rabbit with rice
Beans
Buckwheat pancake
with jam

Day 2
Rice Krispies
Bacon (nitrate free) and
sauté potatoes
Fruit juice or melon

Scallops with cheese
sauce
Bean sprouts
Mashed potato
Natural yoghurt with
honey and grapes*

Bone broth (pork bone)
with pearl barley
Macaroons
Mashed banana

Omelette
Tomato and cress salad
Wholewheat gingerbread
with nuts

Day 3
Muesli with sultanas*
and apple*
Boiled egg with *Ryvita*
and butter

Day 4
Millet porridge
Finnan haddock with
rice
Orange (raw)*

Ox kidney and rice
Turnip
Sago pudding with
stewed apricots*

Potatoes in Irish stew
with pearl barley
Broccoli
Baked banana
Milk jelly

Sausage (pork) and mash
Raw cabbage and
grated carrot salad
'Cow cake'

Soup – bone broth
with onion
Wholewheat toast
and jam
Prunes* or melon

Day 5
Oat Porridge
Dates wrapped in bacon
(nitrate free)
Ryvita, butter and
Marmite

Day 6
Prunes*
Egg and bacon
(nitrate free)
Ryvita with molasses

Pigeon
Roast parsnips
Leeks
Tapioca

Lamb chop
Cabbage
Baked potato
Junket

Raw pear

Herring roes
Grilled tomato*
Wholewheat shortbread
Baked potato

Day 7
Lamb's kidney and bacon
Fruit juice
Pineapple
Oatcakes with Marmite

Chicken with rice
Carrot
Custard
Jam tart (wholewheat)

Potato with cheese
Lettuce and cucumber*
Tapioca walnut pudding
Raw orange*

Day 9
Millet porridge
Scrambled egg and
bacon
Fruit juice
Orange*

Potatoes boiled in
jackets

Stewed apple*
with honey

Fresh mackerel
Tomato and cress salad
Wholewheat bread and
butter, or cake

Day 8
Wholewheat Force or
Sunnybisk
Beef sausage
Raw apple*

Haddock pie
Cauliflower
Rice pudding with prunes

Tongue salad
Beetroot and yoghurt
Mashed banana
'Cow cake'

Day 10
Rice Krispies
Herring
Raw pear

Baked potatoes
Minced beef

Liver, tomatoes* and
onions

Wholewheat sponge
pudding

Marrow*

Rhubarb and tapioca

Bone broth with peas
or lentils

Ryvita with peanut butter

Junket

Baked beans* with
mushrooms

Wholewheat semolina
with sultanas and egg

A 'Safe' Foods List (Winter 1983)

The HACSG have checked the following foods with the
manufacturers to make sure they are free from forbidden
additives. We have tried to list as many useful items as
possible – you may find more if you look carefully at
labels, as all ingredients must be itemized.

Marks & Spencer
Bread – *Allinsons*
Fresh chicken/turkey meats
Peanut butter
Peanuts
Cashew nuts
Pure cooking oil
Grapefruit juice
Natural yoghurt
Grapefruit marmalade
Cream

Sainsbury
Porridge oats, *Wheat Flakes, Corn Flakes, Sunnybisk*
English butter and cheese
Cream
Honey
Pure vegetable fat

Grapefruit/plain yoghurt
*Frozen concentrated lemon drink

Health stores
Losely yoghurt
Barley Cup drink
Castus date and nut bars
Hügli vegetable stock cubes
Pantry Stock gravy mix
Mapleton's Savoury Mix

Flours
Jordans stoneground 85-100%
Allinsons stoneground 85-100%
Marriages stoneground 85-100%
Prewetts wholemeal
Hofels organically grown

Sugars (keep sugar to an absolute minimum)
Billingtons natural Demerara
Billingtons molasses sugar
Billingtons light and dark Muscovado
Sainsburys Muscovado
Prewletts light Muscovado

Other makes
Heinz Treacle/rice/tapioca puddings
Heinz grapefruit and pineapple juices
Jordans golden crunchy cereal
Shreddies, Sunny Bisk, Grapenuts, Shredded Wheat, Shredded Wheat (spoon size), *Sunnybisk*
Golden Wonder plain crisps
Morlands Munch oat biscuits
Eden Vale yoghurt with honey and grapefruit
Elsenham's preserves
Kerrygold butter and cheese
Tesco butter

Country Life butter
Dairylea cheese spread
Thursday Cottage marmalades
Tiptree jams and marmalades
James Keiller marmalades
Marmite, honey
Free-range eggs
Boot's baby porridge/oats/rice cereal/mixed cereal

HACSG would like to point out that the 'Safe' foods list has to be updated every 6 months, so we cannot guarantee that the foods in the list above are still available, or still has the same ingredients.

Fuller and more up-to-date lists are sent out with all copies of the HACSG Diet Booklet.

If your child is able to tolerate some fruits/vegetables with salicylates, the following foods are without colourings and flavourings:

Heinz baked beans/sandwich spread
Heinz tomato soup
*Carnival strawberry jam
*Baby Ribena
*Lanes blackcurrant juice
Keymarket baked beans
Raisins

Things to avoid
Coloured toothpaste, soap, bath bubbles, etc.

Antacids, quinine sulphate (in some cough mixtures)

Aspirin-based products.* *Paracetamol* may be given for headaches but should be kept to a minimum.

Tartrazine (yellow dye) is found in some medicines and tablets.

Septrin. We have had reports that the antibiotic Septrin produces a strong reaction in some children.

RECIPES

Wholewheat bread

3 lb (1.3kg) 100 per cent wholewheat stoneground flour
3 teaspoonsful salt (preferably sea salt)
1 oz (25g) fresh yeast (or ½oz [12g] dried yeast soaked in
   2 tablespoonsful of warm water till softened)
1 teaspoonful dark brown sugar
1 tablespoonful vegetable oil (optional)
Approx. 1½ pints (900ml) of warm water (just hand hot)

Makes 5 1 lb loaves

1. Put flour and salt into a large mixing bowl, and stand it somewhere to get warm, if necessary over a bowl of hot water.

2. Mix yeast and sugar and 2 tablespoonsful warm water and leave in a warm place for about 10 minutes till covered with small bubbles (an airing cupboard will do).

3. Make a hollow in the flour and pour in frothy yeast and oil if used.

4. Add 1½ pints (900ml) warm water and mix well together to make a smooth dough. If the dough is too dry to bind together, add just a little more water and mix in well. The dough should be slightly softer than pastry but not as moist as fruit cake.

5. Put the dough on a well-floured board and knead well, turning the dough round and picking up the edge and pressing this into the centre. Keep on turning the dough and pressing new sides into the centre for about 5 minutes.

6. Put the dough back into the bowl, cover with a damp cloth and leave in a warm place until almost doubled in size (about 30-45 minutes).

7. Preheat oven to 450°F/230°C (Gas Mark 8).

8. Turn risen dough out onto floured board and knead again lightly.

9. Divide into five equal pieces and knead each into shape to fit 1lb tins which should be greased and warmed. If preferred, make four loaves and a batch of rolls.

10. Cover with a cloth and leave in a warm (not hot) place until the dough is about ½ inch above the top of the tin (usually about 30 minutes).

11. Bake at 450°F/230°C (Gas Mark 8) for approximately 30-35 minutes. The loaves should be lightly browned on top, and sound hollow when tapped on the bottom. Rolls will take a shorter time.

12. Put on rack to cool.

Basic cake mixture

This basic mixture will make any type of cake, with nuts, permitted fruits, etc. It will also make a good steamed pudding. If tolerated, chocolate, cinnamon, spices etc. may be added for flavour, as can sultanas,* raisins,* flaked almonds, currants,* chopped dried apricots,* peaches and pears,* glacée pineapple and cashew nuts. Avoid coloured glacée cherries.

4oz (100g) wholewheat flour
4oz (100g) butter
4oz (100g) raw sugar (Barbados or Muscavado)
2 eggs
1 level teaspoonful of baking powder (aluminium and
   colour free)

Cream the butter and sugar and beat well. Add the eggs with a little flour, then gradually fold in the rest of the flour.

For a light sponge, add a heaped teaspoonful of cornflour. Put this on the weighing scales first and then make the flour up to 4oz (100g). Bake at 400°F/200°C (Gas Mark 6) for 15 minutes. Cook for a few minutes longer than for a 'white' recipe.

For a sponge pudding to put on top of fruit, substitute 1½oz (38g) of ground almonds or 1½oz (38g) ground hazelnuts for 1½oz (38g) of flour.

Basic biscuit mixture

1oz (25g) cornflour
7oz (190g) wholewheat flour
4oz (100g) butter
4oz (100g) raw sugar
1 egg
(Can be flavoured with grated lemon rind, or cinnamon if neither affect the child adversely.)

Cream the butter and sugar and beat well. Add egg with a little flour, then gradually fold in rest. Roll out the mixture on a board. Cut into shapes, put on a greased oven sheet and bake in a moderate oven 350°F/180°C (Gas Mark 4) for 10 minutes. Remove and allow to cool, and then replace in the oven for a further 10 minutes, to give a crisper biscuit.

Shortbread

8oz (200g) wholewheat flour
2oz (50g) raw sugar
4oz (100g) butter
(If he is not salicylate-sensitive, use 6oz (150g) flour and 2oz (50g) ground almonds.)

Work sugar into the flour. Then work butter in with the fingers. Press down into buttered sponge tin. Prick centre with a fork, and mark round the edge with a fork. Cook at 350°F/180°C (Gas Mark 4) for about 40 minutes. Do not remove from the tin until cold.

Cow cake
6 oz (150g) rolled oats
4 oz (100g) butter
4 oz (100g) raw cane sugar

Mix all ingredients together, press into a baking tin and cook at 350°F/180°C (Gas Mark 4) for about 25 minutes. Cut into fingers while still hot.

Gingerbread
¼ level teaspoonful bicarbonate of soda
Pinch of salt
1 oz (25g) shredded almonds (substitute equivalent of flour if child is salicylate-sensitive)
2 oz (50g) raw sugar
½-1 teaspoonful ginger   } Find out if child is
½-1 teaspoonful cinnamon } sensitive to these
1 handful of sultanas if tolerated
1 handful of cashew nuts (optional)
4 oz (100g) wholewheat flour
1 oz (25g) pinhead oatmeal
2 oz (50g) molasses
3 oz (75g) butter
1 egg
1 dessertspoonful of water, if required, to mix
1 teaspoonful sunflower seed oil

Mix together all the dry ingredients. Melt together the butter, treacle and mix in with dry ingredients. Add beaten egg. Cook at 350°F/180°C (Gas Mark 4) for about 15 minutes, then turn down and leave in for a further 20 minutes. This gingerbread improves with keeping.

Scones
4 oz (100g) wholewheat flour
1 tablespoonful of wheat germ
1 oz (25g) butter
½ oz (12½g) raw cane sugar
½ level teaspoonful bicarbonate of soda
1 egg
1 teaspoonful of milk (approximately)
Sultanas or currants if tolerated

Put dry ingredients into a bowl and rub in the fat. Add the egg and the milk and mix to a dough. Roll the dough into balls and pat to approximately ½ inch flat. Pop in a hot oven – 450°F/230°C (Gas Mark 8) – for about 8-10 minutes.

Gluten-free sponge cake
4 oz (100g) butter
4 oz (100g) raw sugar
2 eggs
½ oz (12½g) cornflour
2 oz (50g) rice flour
2 oz (50g) potato flour
Pinch of salt
1 rounded teaspoonful of home-made baking powder

Cream the butter and sugar and beat well. Add the eggs. Mix the dry ingredients in bowl and then fold in gradually. Bake in greased sandwich tins in a preheated oven – 400°F/200°C (Gas Mark 6) for 15 minutes.

Gluten-free scones
4 heaped tablespoonsful *Jubilee* bread mix
1½ heaped tablespoonsful gluten-free muesli base
1 rounded tablespoonful raw sugar
½ teaspoonful bicarbonate of soda
2oz (50g) butter or margarine
1-2 tablespoonsful milk

Put dry ingredients in a bowl and mix well. Rub in butter, and mix in milk to make a damp dough. Form into little rounds, place on a greased baking tray and bake in a hot oven – 400°F/200°C (Gas Mark 6) – for 8-9 minutes.

Gluten-free little cakes
4oz (100g) butter
4oz (100g) raw sugar
1½oz (37½g) yellow pea flour
1½oz (37½g) brown rice flour
1½oz (37½g) polenta
2 eggs
1 level teaspoonful cream of tartar
½ level teaspoonful bicarbonate of soda
Nuts or permitted fruits or flavourings

Follow method for sponge cake and divide the mixture into patty pans. Bake in a preheated oven 400°F/200°C (Gas Mark 6) for 15 minutes.

Notes

[1] Organically-grown vegetables are available from some health food stores. The Organic Food Service, The Soil Association, and The Foresight Association can all provide addresses of places which sell organically-grown food (see p.125).

[2] See note 1 above for details of sources of meat from organic farms.

3
ALLERGIES

In recent years, allergy is believed to have surpassed infection as the main cause of illness. Although sensitivity to substances such as pollen and animal fur has long been recognized, the wider implications of chemical pollution and food additives are now beginning to be understood. Contact dermatitis from washing powders and other skin irritations such as rashes, eczema, psoriasis, sweating, are old news. Chemical irritation of the mucous membranes leads to mouth ulcers, sneezing, asthma, hay fever – which takes the form of running eyes and nose, or stomach discomfort, colitis or bloating and diarrhoea in coeliac disease. What is new, is that allergic reactions can cause a whole group of mental and emotional problems, a common one for example being simply a feeling of continual fatigue. The child in chronic discomfort is more likely to be restless, whiney and hyperactive.

Medical people argue as to whether these adverse reactions to foods and inhaled substances should be called allergic reactions, intolerances or food sensitivities. Whatever name is given to the problem, the solution is the same – avoid the incriminated substance.

Allergies and hyperactivity
Almost any allergen can cause hyperactivity in a susceptible child. Hyperactive children have highly sensitive nervous systems, which would explain why in a family which eats the same food only one child becomes a victim. Children

who are allergically sensitive to food are often also sensitive to inhaled allergens. They might perhaps only be *seasonally* hyperactive at the time that grass and trees are pollenating. Other common allergens are cigarette smoke, car and diesel exhaust fumes, animal dandruff, effluent from North Sea gas and hydrocarbons from plastics. Where possible the suspected source should be removed for a short period to confirm or deny the connection. Allergic reactions are more common in the poor feeder who may have nutritional deficiencies which lead to inadequacies of the immune system; and the child who was given artificial feeding at an early age.

How Do Allergies Start?

Nutrient deficiencies in the mother

An American study[1] on cats has produced evidence to suggest that trace mineral deficiencies in the mother produced kittens with allergies.

In a study at Charing Cross Hospital[2] in London, Dr Ellen Grant found that, in adults, smoking and the contraceptive pill increased the chances of food allergy. Smoking is known to increase levels of cadmium and lead and decrease levels of zinc, and vitamin B complex, C and E. The pill is known to decrease levels of zinc, manganese, vitamins B_6, B_2, B_{12} and C. By increasing excretion of vitamin B_6 in the urine, zinc deficiency would reduce levels of nicotinamide (made in the intestine with the help of B_6 and B_2) and plasma vitamin A.

It is, therefore, possible that children born to women who smoke or who have recently discontinued the pill, will be lacking in these nutrients and therefore more allergy prone, as these essential nutrients are needed for the production of enzymes necessary to metabolize food correctly, and for optimal adrenal function.

Early feeding habits

Adverse reactions may be brought on by too early an introduction of cow's milk, sugar, supplements such as orange juice or fish-liver oils, vitamin drops containing artificial colouring and flavouring, and even solid feeding. A baby's immature digestive tract is prepared only for breast milk in the first five to six months of life.

Food additives

Another problem is, as we have seen, the introduction of 'foreign bodies' into our diet. 'Food additives' are, in reality, anything but food – 'non-food' additives would be a better description! According to Dr Ben Feingold, the body may detoxify these additives by coating them in a substance the body tolerates, such as zinc, and then passing them out via the liver or kidneys. Thus, over a period of time, they squander body reserves of zinc or other protective nutrients.

Nutritional deficiencies in the child

Yet another theory is that due to deficiencies, the lining of the intestine breaks down and becomes more porous, letting through substances into the blood which should have been further broken down before passing across the intestinal wall.

Pollution

Another problem is believed to be that lead, chlorine, North Sea gas, fluoride and other pollutants inhibit the production of enzymes, as does a paucity of the nutrients the body needs. Indoor gas boilers can cause considerable pollution.

These theories do not, in fact, conflict. The baby in the womb whose trace mineral nourishment has been minimal, is the baby from the poorly-nourished mother in whom lactation may easily fail. Once the mother finds herself short of breast-milk, she must resort to unnatural and unsuitable substances to try to satisfy the infant's demands. Cow's milk, sugar, orange juice, fish-liver oil and an assortment of cereals may shortly assault the infant's delicate digestive tract, causing metabolic chaos and possibly malabsorption.

The injured intestinal tract may allow undigested particles of food to pass through into the circulating blood: vital trace minerals may not be absorbed, vital intestinal flora may be superseded by unpropitious flora which may encourage the growth of unwanted bacteria, which in turn may sap the baby's strength. Vitamin and mineral deficiencies may then abound.

Added to these problems is the fact that with every breath the child takes he may inhale lead, traffic exhaust fumes, cigarette smoke, hydrocarbons, outgassing from plastics, and effluent from factories and/or North Sea gas. With every mouthful he eats or drinks, he may take in lead, copper and/or aluminium contamination, a plethora of chemical additives, and a number of foods to which his body has become sensitized as a result of too-early weaning. It is hardly surprising he has a problem!

Positive Action

1. Introduce a good, wholefood diet of foods he can tolerate (we discussed this in Chapter 2).

2. Remove toxic metals and supplement necessary trace elements (see Chapter 4).

3. Identify and eliminate substances he cannot tolerate.

Identifying food allergies
If, after having introduced a good wholefood diet, the child is not very much improved in eight weeks, it is worth going to some trouble to pinpoint possible allergies. The first step may be to look back and see if you can remember when the hyperactivity/screaming/night-

waking/diarrhoea/eczema/asthma or whatever started. If it was (as it so often is) when he/she was weaned off the breast onto cow's milk, and you suspect that your child may have an allergy or intolerance of cow's milk, it is important that you seek professional advice, either from your doctor, or community dietician (at the local hospital).

Eliminating cow's milk for a few weeks, and then re-introducing it again, may cause *severe* problems, if the child has an 'undiagnosed' intolerance to cow's milk.

If he was weaned early but seemed happy on the bottle, he may have adapted successfully to the cow's milk, and the next stumbling block may be the introduction of cereals. If he was introduced to cereals before four-and-a-half to five months, he may well have had diarrhoea, or been restless, grizzly and unable to settle. If this continued, he may have a grain allergy. Citrus allergy, started by a bad reaction to the orange juice, may also be easy to spot.

If the allergies seemed to develop later in life, when he was taking a wide variety of foods, then it may be more difficult to pinpoint the specific food or foods. Many children have three or four allergic foods, a few have even more. Sometimes the reaction does not come for some hours, which makes it quite hard to identify, but with perseverance you can win through.

The second idea is to keep a 'food diary' for a few weeks, writing down everything the child eats, and when he has a particularly 'bad turn'. If the problem is something he only eats occasionally, such as tomatoes or chocolate, this method of detection will often be successful. If, on the other hand, it is a very common food such as milk, eggs or wheat, which he eats every day, this approach will probably not reveal very much.

If your doctor is quite sympathetic it is possible to get tests done, and sometimes these are very helpful (and will probably confirm what you already suspected), but only a limited number of foods will be tested, and none of the ways of testing is 100 per cent reliable.

The other option is to try the child on the rotation diet (given on p.70) for two or three weeks. It is a great bore, but it really does show up the allergies as nothing else can. The child takes each food once a week only, and the reaction will be sharper as the child will have gone without this food for a week. (The other alternative is the 'Caveman Diet' on p.111).

While nobody wants to restrict a young child's diet unnecessarily, the benefits of freeing the child from the detrimental effects of the food he is sensitive to, make it worth removing the offending food from his diet completely for at least several years, in some cases maybe for life.

If a major food is to be excluded from the diet, it is important to check to see which vitamins and minerals would have been present in this food, and to compensate accordingly. For example, milk is high in minerals and vitamins A and D; so if he is not to have milk, he will need plenty of bone broth, possibly bonemeal or dolomite tablets, and plenty of green vegetables. If he can take fish-liver oil this will compensate for the vitamins. If he has to go without grain he will need all the minerals, the B complex vitamins and vitamin E. If your child cannot eat wheat or tolerate cow products, you may feel your problems have only just begun. On p.114 we give suggestions for wheat-free, milk-free, gluten-free diets, and on p.115 there is a list of useful recipe books. If your doctor is sympathetic he may put you in touch with a dietitian who will be able to give you further help.

Coeliac disease

In cases of coeliac disease (malabsorption due to sensitivity to the gluten grains – wheat, oats, barley and rye) there has usually been a history of loose stools, or big bulky stools, probably passed several times a day since early childhood. Sometimes these stools are very pale; sometimes they are full of undigested food; sometimes the child has long bouts of diarrhoea which are quite difficult to stop – especially when teething.

The child is thin, hyperactive, easily tired, very prone to tears and tantrums, talkative and overexcitable. Pant- and bed-wetting is common and sleeping is usually poor. He may complain of abdominal pain or rectal cramp.

A good idea is to give the child a diet which contains no flour products and cereals for about four weeks to see if the symptoms abate. If so, it is worth asking your GP to examine the child for coeliac disease.

A Rotated Diet for the Detection of Allergy

The rotated diet on p.70 is designed to give each specific food only one day in seven. The diet eliminates the most common allergens – cow's milk, grains and eggs – also all stimulants such as coffee, tea, chocolate and sugar.

Where possible all four foods listed should be taken at each meal and no drink should be taken except the juice of the day and water. All goods must be boiled in plain water, steamed, grilled or cooked in the oven in a covered dish. No fats, oils, gravies are to be used. During the trial period no food other than those listed may be taken at all.

During the first week of the diet adverse reactions may take place due to the withdrawal of cow's milk, etc. if these are allergic substances. For a few days the reactions may be quite strong – akin to the alcoholic withdrawal in the first few days of abstinence.

The food can be taken in various ways. Tuesday's breakfast could be grilled pork slice; lunch a pork chop; supper slices from a pork joint. On Wednesdays, breakfast could be lamb's kidneys: lunch could be a lamb chop and the evening meal could be lamb's liver. Beef could be alternated with veal, brains, ox-tail, ox-tongue, etc.

Unfinished food of the day should be put in the freezer for the following week. If only fruit and vegetables which will be consumed on the day are bought, it removes

A rotated diet

Monday	Tuesday	Wednesday	Thursday	Friday	Saturday	Sunday
Chicken	Pork	Lamb	Turkey	Fish	Rabbit	Beef
Banana	Sago	Brown rice	Maize (sweetcorn)	Millet	Lentils	Potato
Pineapple	Dates	Orange	Cornflour	Millet flakes	Green beans	Tomato
Beetroot	Apple	Grapefruit	Leeks	Cabbage	Peas	Aubergine
Spinach	Pear	Satsuma	Onions	Savoy cabbage	Black-eyed beans	Cucumber
Swiss chard	Lettuce	Mandarin	Asparagus	Brussels sprouts	Broad beans	Marrow
Pineapple juice	Endive	Lime	Chives	Broccoli	Mung bean shoots	Melon
	Chicory	Carrot	Grapes	Cauliflower	Plums	Tomato juice
	Artichoke	Celery	Sultanas	Kohlrabi	Peaches	
	Sunflower seeds	Parsnip	Grape juice	Swedes	Apricot	
	Apple juice	Parsley		Avocado	Cherry	
		Orange or grapefruit juice		Figs	Prunes	
				Water	Prune juice	

temptation for the following day. The child may be more hungry than usual, however, and it is important to have enough food available.

The diet will have ensured six days without the offending food so the reaction to the allergen will probably be fairly immediate and take the form of a running or stuffed-up nose, headache, stomach pain, feeling of bloatedness, extreme lethargy, irritability, etc. The day this occurs can be marked on the diet sheet. It is then possible to test the foods eaten on this day one at a time.

Having thus worked out a basic diet of 'safe' foods, it will then be possible to test common allergens, such as cow's milk, eggs, the gluten grains – wheat, oats, barley, rye – and other fruits. After three weeks' abstinence the reaction may be strong, so at first only a small quantity of the substance should be given. If the reaction is very severe, a teaspoonful of bicarbonate of soda in water will help to alleviate the symptoms. Have a glass of this with you.

After an adverse reaction a return to known safe foods for a few days will be necessary before testing for another possible allergen. After a few weeks it should be possible to identify all food allergies in this way.

Identifying Inhaled Allergens

Again detective work is needed. The types of questions you may need to ask are:

Is he worse in the winter? If so, do you have a gas fire on in the winter but not in the summer?

Does he react more in heavy traffic than in the park or indoors?

Does he 'go silly' after playing with the cat or dog?

Is he worse in certain rooms where there are plastic-covered chairs/a coal fire?

The HACSG has found the following inhaled allergens commonly affect children: household cleaners and polishes, aerosols, hair sprays and perfumes, felt-tip pens, fly killers, solid air fresheners and insecticides and coloured bubble bath. Once you know the type of thing to look for the picture may be clarified surprisingly quickly. 'He's always been really bad in the car – especially in the town I've noticed'; 'When he's been with the horses, he seems to go beserk and then fall asleep'; 'He was so much better all summer, then it all started again in September – it must have been when we started using the gas fire again', are some of the observations which will help pinpoint the problem.

Identifying Very Difficult Cases

The conventional 'skin tests' and 'sublingual [under the tongue!] drop' tests have their uses with the very difficult cases. There are some excellent doctors working with allergy on both sides of the Atlantic and if spending a few weeks in careful observation and manipulating the diet fails to come up with a clear-cut answer, it may be worth finding a doctor who can help with the detection work. (HACSG and Foresight can supply addresses.)

'Growing Out' of Allergies

As the child's system is rested from dealing with foods to which he reacts badly, the intestinal tract may heal, and the beneficial intestinal flora increase in number, so that the child's general health is improved. Supplements of vitamin A, B complex, and zinc help both this healing process and the development of the enzyme systems because as the body level of beneficial trace minerals increases, 'enemies' such as lead will be excreted which will improve the chances of enzyme activity. This is why the 'allergies' may be 'grown out of' as the child's health improves.

With the coeliac child, evidence to date seems to suggest that the problem is life-long, but with other less virulent allergies, it may be possible to reintroduce the foods after a year or so – perhaps in small quantities and at stated intervals only. This will be a matter for you and your child to discuss and observe together. The older children get, the easier it is for them to co-operate. At eight or nine they can be surprisingly wise about their own reactions. If there is a bad reaction, however, this should be noted and the food discontinued again. When the episode is over it helps to discuss the way the food/fumes etc. affected him and recognize the connection. In this way your child will become involved in his health problem and can start to play a positive part in treating it.

Notes

[1] Dr Frank Pottenger of the Price Pottenger Association, PO Box 2614, La Mesa, California 92041.

[2] See Dr Ellen Grant (1979) Food allergies and migraine *The Lancet* 1, 1, p.966; (1981) article in *The International Journal of Environmental Studies* 17, 1, p.57-66.

4
HEAVY METAL TOXICITIES, TRACE MINERAL IMBALANCE AND HAIR ANALYSIS

In the 1980s we live in a constantly changing and increasingly hazardous environment. Many pollutants that the adult body may have learned to cope with, detoxify and discard, are a danger to the health and development of small children, so the modern parent has to become increasingly vigilant to protect the child's well-being. It is now part of our job as parents to become informed about harmful substances children are likely to come in contact with and take positive action.

Heavy Metal Toxicities

Recently a number of important developments in lead research have contributed to the body of evidence linking lead levels in children tested in several industrialized countries to behavioural problems and IQ deficits ... It is generally accepted that children are particularly at risk from lead exposure because of the specific metabolic conditions of childhood, and the vulnerability of the developing nervous system.[1]

In her work with 'mentally disturbed' children,[2] a Californian paediatrician, Dr Elizabeth Lodge-Rees, has found them to be disadvantaged both emotionally and mentally not only by a high body-burden of lead but also by cadmium, mercury, aluminium and excess copper or selenium. She wrote: 'These children may have many minor health problems, allergic syndromes, hyperactivity, dyslexia, learning difficulties or in many cases just poor school records and a persistent inability to "fit in" with the day-to-day demands of normal life.'

Lead

The lead content of the air we breathe has risen sharply, due partly to the higher lead content of petrol and partly to the increase in car ownership in post-war Britain.

Studies from this country, America, Australia and Switzerland have correlated the high body-lead with hyperactivity and learning difficulties, with congenital anomaly of the central nervous system, with stillbirth and with cancer.

Professor Lawther recently headed a group of government scientists who brought out a report entitled *Lead and Health*[3] which queried the validity of all these studies. In November 1980, Professor Bryce-Smith of Reading University and Dr R. Stephens of Birmingham University published a reply entitled *Lead or Health*.[4] We suggest parents who would like to study the question for themselves read both these reports.

What *is* beyond question is that 76,000 tonnes of lead are emitted from car exhausts every year. This lead is circulating in the air we breathe, the dust in our houses, and landing on food crops, soil, water and grazing land. Also beyond question is that the worst areas of lead pollution are the urban areas where the traffic is thickest,[5] and that there are more hyperactive children in towns and cities than there are in rural areas.

Dr Billick also did a study in America showing that the blood levels of lead in city children rose and fell with the seasonal variation in the amount of leaded petrol sold at the petrol stations. The graph indicates how exactly the lead levels in the children followed the amount of leaded petrol sold in the vicinity where they lived.

Traffic fumes are not the only source of lead in the

environment. A great number of households in this country have lead levels in the drinking water above that permitted by the World Health Organization. Lead in the drinking water has been correlated by Dr Michael Moore of Glasgow with mental retardation in babies. The higher the lead in the maternal drinking water, the greater the degree of mental retardation in the baby.

Some food tins have lead seams, and this lead may seep into the food. (In most Continental countries, and in Australia they make seamless tins.)

Flaking leaded-paint is frequently quoted as a source of lead in small children. This seems unlikely as not many mothers allow their children to eat paint continuously! But in rare cases, if decoration is in a very bad state of repair, this might be a source of lead.

Without doubt the most widespread source of lead in children is lead in petrol – either inhaled directly from traffic fumes or from contaminated food. The addresses of a number of pressure groups campaigning against lead in petrol are given on p.125.

Children with dark skins may absorb toxic metals more readily due to possible difficulties with calcium metabolism.

Copper

In soft-water areas the copper used in plumbing may leach into the drinking water. In many areas the water contains both lead and copper, the lead having come from the pipes under the road leading to the house and/or lead-glazed mains. Where the lead pipe leading to the house joins the copper pipe there is a type of electrical charge that causes the copper to leach lead from the lead pipe. Particularly at risk are soft water areas where the water is acid as a result of an acid peaty-type soil. This acidity tends to leach metal from the plumbing into the water. The baby having an early morning bottle is especially vulnerable because the kettle will be filled with water that has stood in the pipe overnight, and therefore contains a greater amount of both lead and copper than any other water drunk subsequently during the day.

Copper sulphate is used in swimming pools to kill algae so if a child has a high copper hair analysis after swimming regularly in such a pool, the reading could be false. Another sample should be checked six weeks after he has stopped swimming.

Aluminium

The main source of aluminium is thought to be cooking pans and food cooked in foil. It is also found in substances such as *Coffee-Mate*, *Compliment*, *Gelusil* and some salts and baking powders. As ever, read the labels on these products carefully and change to another brand if necessary. Very high aluminium levels have been found in people who use aluminium pressure-cookers and kettles.

Cadmium

The main source of cadmium is parental cigarette smoke. Most hyperactive children have been found to improve when their parents stop smoking. Some cadmium can be obtained from alloys used in plumbing – yet again the soft water areas are more vulnerable.

Mercury

Mercury apparently comes from fish, but as all seed wheat is dusted with mercury before sowing, it seems feasible that some may find its way into the drinking water where the rain has washed off the wheat fields into gullies and thence to the rivers. There is little that can be done about this. There is no reason to stop eating fish because it is not often contaminated. In any event high mercury is not a frequent problem.

Selenium

Over-high selenium is usually the result of too-frequent use of selenium-containing shampoos, unsufficient rinsing and using in the bath, etc. Detailed warnings are given on the bottles/wrappings of such shampoos but are sometimes ignored. To avoid confused interpretation, the hair should not be tested until six weeks after discontinuing the use of the shampoo.

Trace Mineral Imbalance

Most minerals are better absorbed in the presence of vitamin C, the B complex vitamins and/or the essential fatty acids and vitamin E, so ideally it is best to give the mineral supplements as part of a vitamin and mineral supplementation programme.

The following vitamins should be supplied with the minerals:

calcium	vitamin D
magnesium	nicotinamide; B_6 and D
iron	vitamin C
copper	vitamin A
manganese	choline, B_6, pantothenate, biotin, folate, evening primrose oil, vitamin E
Zinc	vitamin B_6, *Cantassium FF-E* capsules vitamin B_6, *Cantassium FF-E* capsules (they contain evening primrose oil and vitamin E)
chromium	vitamin B_1 and nicotinamide
selenium	vitamin E

Cobalt deficiencies
Vitamin B_{12} can be used alone to counteract cobalt deficiency. The vitamin B_{12} in *Junomac* is usually sufficient but check this in subsequent hair analyses.

Low sodium and potassium levels
It is often helpful to give vitamins A, C and E and B complex, particularly pantothenic acid and nicotinamide.

These vitamins assist the adrenal glands to function and this in turn helps to combat the tendency to allergic syndromes. Stressed adrenal function leads to sodium/ potassium imbalance.

Junomac supplement

Junomac (see p.44) provides dolomite (for calcium and magnesium), manganese, zinc and chromium with vitamins A, B, C, D and E and evening primrose oil for essential fatty acids. It does not contain artificial colourings, preservatives, gluten, sugar or cane products. *Junomac* has been designed so that the correct supplement is one tablet per stone in bodyweight. It is suitable for children up to six stone in weight.

Iron deficiency

Junoiron contains iron, a trace of copper and the vitamin C necessary for the absorption of the iron (see p.79). Like *Junomac* it is non-allergic. This has also been designed so that the child has one daily per stone of body weight. If iron levels are just slightly low, raisins soaked in lemon juice* all day and eaten in the evening are a good source of iron. It is best to give iron in the evenings. Other minerals should be given at breakfast for maximum absorption. If the child has over-high copper, 1 iron orotate per three stone in body weight can be used (or a suitable fraction, i.e., ⅓ tablet per stone in body weight) with a pinch of vitamin C powder in his drink.

Brewer's yeast

Cheaper, but less detailed supplementation, can be given with brewer's yeast (for those who are *not* yeast sensitive) and halibut-liver oil, either the liquid or in capsules. This, however, does not give the evening primrose oil and vitamin E which has been found to be so helpful.

Hair analysis

One method of screening to get an indication of whether a child has a high level of toxic metals and/or deficiencies of essential minerals is by hair analysis.

To obtain a hair sample, two tablespoonsful of hair should be taken from the back of the head. It can be taken in small snippets from different places, so in most cases it will not be obvious that it has been cut at all. The sample should be taken from as close to the scalp as possible and each tuft should be not longer than 35mm. Send a large (9in x 6in) S.A.E. to either the HACSG or the Foresight Association requesting the application forms for a hair analysis. While treating for metal toxicities and/or deficiencies of trace minerals, the hair should be tested at least once every six weeks.

There are a few typical aberrant patterns that turn up time and again on the hair analyses.

Poor diet

The first and easiest to recognize is the curve of a child who has been on an inadequate diet and probably had a very poor appetite, except for sweets and sugary 'junk' food. This chart will often show a very high calcium level (possibly from the chalk in white bread) but other trace minerals – magnesium, iron, copper, zinc, manganese, chromium, selenium and cobalt – may be low right across the chart. If there are no toxic metals present, these children will respond to a diet rich in essential nutrients – whole grains, raw fruit and vegetables, and a course of *Junomac* and *Junoiron*. (If the child is salicylate-sensitive, ask for 'cider free' *Junomac*).

In such cases the problem is *outside* rather than *inside* the child. The poor appetite will respond to the supplementation. If the zinc level is very low (below 12mg%) give *Cantassium*, zinc and vitamin B_6 drops, one drop per day per 10lbs of body weight for a few months.

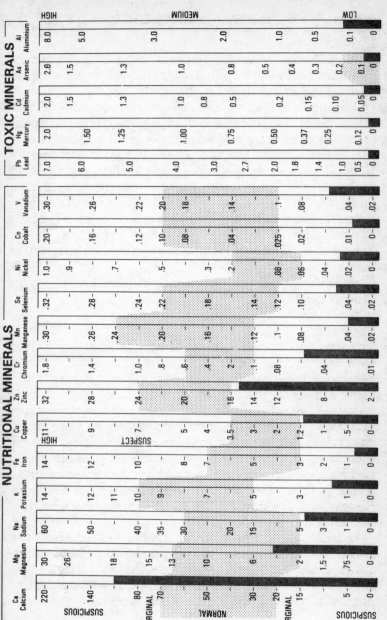

Figure 1   A typical chart of a child on a refined diet, but living in an unpolluted area

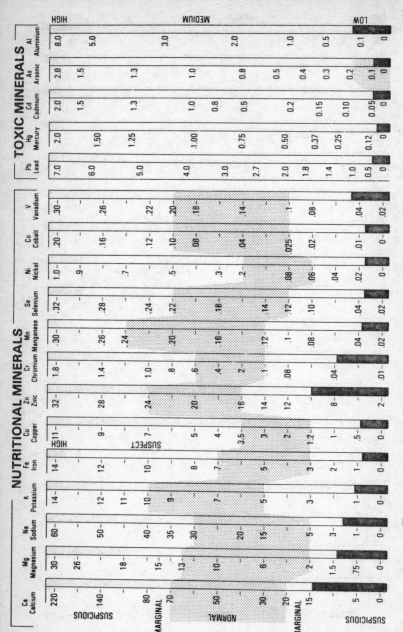

Figure 2 A typical chart of a child with malabsorption syndrome

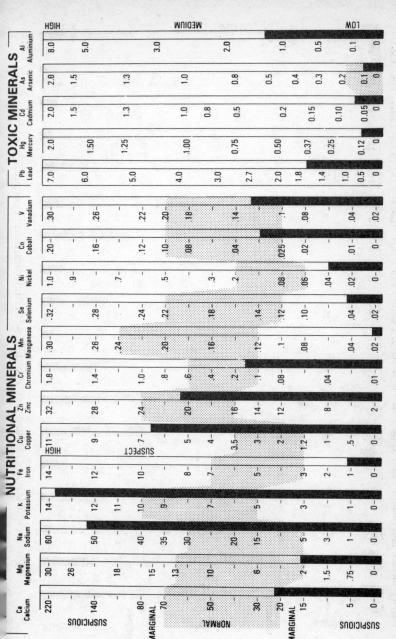

Figure 3 A typical chart of a child with heavy metal toxicity

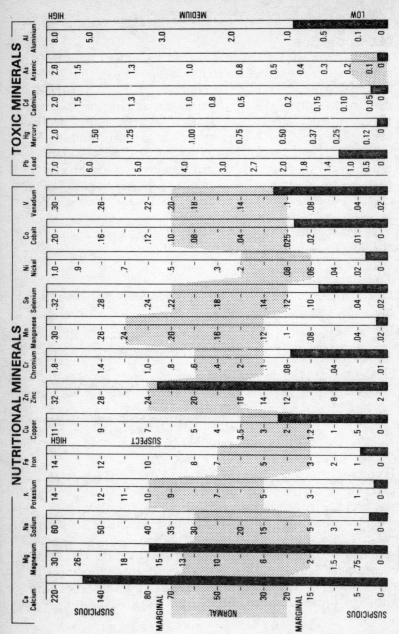

Figure 4 A typical chart of a child with low sodium and potassium levels

Malabsorption

Another common pattern is that of the child low in *all* (or almost all) minerals down to halfway between the shaded areas and the bottom of the column, or even lower. This usually indicates malabsorption or infestation such as threadworms. The latter can usually be detected just by asking the child if his bottom itches at night, and can be cured by powders prescribed by a GP. Pants, pyjamas, etc. should be washed in disinfectant and/or boiled to prevent re-infestation, and trousers should be washed or cleaned. Bedding and duvet covers will need to be cleaned as well.

Malabsorption may be due to coeliac disease or milk allergy (see Chapter 3).

Toxic metals

Low mineral patterns may be seen in combination with a high toxic metal pattern, as a low level of zinc and/or manganese tends to make the child more prone to accumulating toxic metals, and high levels of lead etc. can drive manganese out of the body. The toxic metals can be cleansed from the body with *Garlimac* (a *Cantassium* product) available from health food stores or from The Cantassium Company (see Useful Addresses).

The Cleansing Programme

If you require help, the HACSG and Foresight Association can supply addresses of doctors who are experienced in this field. Please enclose a S.A.E. with your request.

Before starting the cleansing programme it is vital to make sure the trace minerals are well up into the normal range. This is because the preparations used for cleansing remove *all* minerals and metals, not just the harmful ones, and it is very important for the child not to become short of those that are needed.

The first twelve weeks

Give *Junomac* with breakfast and *Junoiron* with evening meals. If any mineral is particularly low, give an additional orotate tablet of that specific mineral, with the vitamins necessary for absorption. For low calcium and magnesium give one 500mg dolomite tablet per five stone in body weight. For low zinc give *Cantassium* zinc and B_6 drops (3.5mg zinc/7mg B_6) one drop per day per 10lbs in body weight. For manganese deficiency give one *Mangamac* tablet (8mg manganese) per three stone in body weight. For chromium deficiency give one chromium orotate tablet per three stone in body weight. For selenium deficiency give one 50mcg selenium tablet per three stone in body weight. Cobalt deficiency may be covered by the B_{12} present in *Junomac*.

How long the mineral supplements will be necessary will depend on how low the minerals registered on the chart. If any mineral was very low indeed, it would be advisable to have another hair test to check it was up to at least nearly normal levels before starting a cleansing programme.

The following four to six weeks

Continue with *Junomac* supplementation in the mornings and give *Garlimac* and *Junoiron* on alternate evenings. Use one *Garlimac* per three stone in body weight. Do not give *Garlimac* for more than ten weeks without retesting the hair.

After the cleansing programme has finished continue with the *Junomac* and *Junoiron* and a pinch of vitamin C powder in juice for eight weeks. Then retest the hair.

If the child has a very high lead level it may be necessary to repeat the cleansing programme several times, as lead is the most difficult metal to shift and seems to be the quickest to return. Lead (like other toxic metals) may, at first, rise in the hair before falling as it is excreted into the hair as it is drawn out of the bone and tissues. Later it will fall quite rapidly as it starts to leave the body. Early in the programme, pant and bed-wetting may be marked in children prone to these, but once the toxic metals are out of the system, this problem will quickly disappear once and for all. This is why school holidays are a good time for cleansing programmes.

Allergies

A very low level of sodium and potassium has been found to be associated with allergies. Dr Elizabeth Lodge-Rees believes that this indicates poor adrenal function which results in lack of a balancing factor called aldosterone (which is made in the adrenals). This pattern has been found to respond to supplementation with vitamins A, E, C and B complex, and removal of the specific allergens. Such a pattern nearly always indicates allergy. (For ways of coping with food and other allergies see Chapter 3.)

Over-high potassium

Children with a high toxic metal level very often also have an extremely high level of potassium. These children are often bed-wetters. When the high toxic metal is removed the potassium settles to a normal level and bed-wetting often ceases.

Epilepsy

Foresight clinicians using hair analysis have found a very low level of manganese always seems to be present in epileptics, with or without a high toxic metal. Fits have been found to improve when the toxic metal (if present) is removed and the manganese level restored with *Mangamac*. Provided the ratio of one *Mangamac* to three stone in body weight is kept to there should be no danger of excessive manganese. The hair should be checked at least every six months.

For children who are hyperactive and epileptic it is recommended that parents get in touch with HACSG or

Foresight for advice before starting the programme.

Over-high copper

Excessive copper can be reduced very easily but it is important *not* to embark on a copper reducing programme if the child is a regular swimming pool 'goer' as it may be exogenously derived. A cleaning therapy using *Garlimac* can bring down the copper level at the rate of approximately 1mg% per week. This should be carefully marked out onto the chart. According to how many mgs of copper need to be cleansed give *Garlimac* every day for up to eight weeks. The same safeguards apply as with lead, levels of beneficial minerals should be brought up to normal before copper reduction is started, i.e. manganese should be seen to be within the normal range. After discontinuing *Garlimac* therapy allow eight weeks on vitamin and mineral supplementation for the hair to grow out before retesting. It is important not to let the copper get too low so the hair analysis should be repeated when the programme is complete.

Aluminium and cadmium

Aluminium and cadmium vary very much in different people and are not very predictable. *Do not cleanse for more than eight weeks*, every other evening. Then grow out the hair for another eight weeks and retest.

Water checks

If you have lead pipes or tank, or if your water is very soft, it is probably worth asking your local water board to test the drinking water at tap-flow for lead, copper, cadmium and aluminium. If your water is above the WHO limit in any of the heavy metals it is important to use a water filter (either a *Mayrei* or *Brita*). The carbon filter should be changed regularly once a month. In heavily contaminated areas the water should be tested again after filtration.

If the child has not been taken to see the family doctor, the parents should do so before embarking on a self-help régime to be sure that nothing else is wrong.

Notes

[1] Jeannie Peterson, article in *Ambio* 8, 5.

[2] Dr Elizabeth Lodge Rees, The Rees Medical Centre, 1511 North Carson Street, PO Box 2768, Carson City, Nevada 89701, USA.

[3] *Lead and Health* (The Lawther Report) HMSO, 1980.

[4] Professor D. Bryce-Smith *Lead or Health?* Conservation Society 1980, available from CALIP, 68 Dora Road, London SW19 7HH.

[5] See I. H. Billick, A. S. Curran, D. R. Shier *Relation of pediatric blood levels to lead in gasolene* HUD Report (1979), The Environmental Research Group, Department of Housing and Urban Development, Washington DC 20410, USA.

[6] Dr Michael Moore, The Gardner Institute for Child Health, Glasgow.

5

DAY-TO-DAY MANAGEMENT OF THE HYPERACTIVE CHILD

Much has been written in recent years about the day-to-day management of the hyperactive child. However, most of the literature seems to be directed at the parents of the physiologically normal but 'difficult' child rather than at the parents of the child whose biochemistry throws up a set of reactions which are entirely different from those of the normal child. So what follows are our suggestions, borne of the experience of living and coping with hyperactive children. While the hyperactivity persists (and treatment may take months rather than weeks) the most important thing is to keep conflict to a minimum and keep a constant check on the child's safety.

The anger and frustration a parent inevitably feels at times while coping with the completely atypical behaviour of the hyperactive child should be directed at those truly responsible. For example, at the Government who, knowing the harm that airborne lead does to children, will still not even *reduce* the lead content of petrol until 1985; at the food manufacturers who still persist in using food colourants and flavourings banned in many other countries, and at the water authorities for providing contaminated water, and at the school caterers who, because of financial cutbacks, do not always encourage wholesome eating habits.

While the child is still hyperactive any reaction will be exaggerated. Where a normal child might not want to do something, the hyperactive child will refuse point blank and have a tantrum if pressed! Where a normal child may just pick up a bright toy, the hyperactive child may put it in his mouth, like a much younger child. Visitors, treats and outings that delight the normal child will result in overexcitement and uncontrollably wild behaviour with the hyperactive child.

The hyperactive child's parents must be constantly on the alert to avoid danger. If the child sees something that attracts him on the other side of the road, he may dash across, oblivious of the traffic. If he sees something on a high shelf, he will climb up to get it with complete disregard of house rules or safety. He may fall off furniture; if windows are left unguarded he may fall out. With any hyperactive child, doors and gates must be made secure; windows, fires and ovens guarded; gas-taps, water-taps, switches and power points covered and guarded as closely as possible, until a much later age than with the normal child.

The hyperactive child cannot remember instructions. A firm 'No' is forgotten within hours, let alone days. Because his brain becomes intensely overstimulated by any mental exertion, instructions of any kind tend to evoke a wild and uncontrolled response. Telling a hyper-active five-year-old to put his vest on may just result in him rushing round the room, waving his vest wildly. Pressure may make him lie on the floor kicking and giggling. Anger will mean tears and tantrums, even fighting, biting or scratching, but it will not make him put his vest on!

If you can see it is a bad day (and days do vary) treat him as you would a much younger child and simply talk to him about other things to distract him while you dress him. Note what he had to eat the previous day, and accept that today he is not well enough to behave at a five-year-old level. This will make things easier for both of you. Trying to 'battle through' and 'make him see sense' while he is full of an allergic substance or toxin simply won't work, and the wear and tear on your nerves and his make it positively harmful.

Another problem area is sitting at the table. If you ask him to use a spoon or just to 'eat up' on a bad day, it may make him jump down and run round the table or disappear underneath it! Instead, simply pick up the spoon and feed him. Again note the previous meal and/or outside factors such as 'Is the gas fire on?', 'Has he been in the car?', 'Has he been exposed to cigarette smoke?' Remember, hyperactivity is an illness which affects behaviour and it is a problem with a solution. Try to blame the allergen or toxin, not the child.

Taking turns with other children is another difficult lesson. He may fight for first turn, the red counter, the mug with picture, and to go on the slide again as soon as he reaches the bottom. Other children's rights must be respected and he *must* be restrained, but expect a violent reaction – it is typical of hyperactivity, not just of your child.

Be prepared to repeat many, many more times, all the edicts and instructions the normal child learns and remembers quite quickly.

Most hyperactive children do not respond to the voice alone. This is not deliberately ignoring the parent, but because they do not process incoming information in the normal way. Even the sound of their own name, repeated several times, may not get a response. Try touching the child to attract his attention. Get him to look at you and focus his attention on you before you speak. Shouting at him will produce more confusion in his brain and may make him run off or have a tantrum.

For the hyperactive child a sharp tap on the wrist or buttock is often the most effective way of making a point that simply *has* to be made. Running across the road, throwing stones at windows or passing cars, dropping milk bottles or pot plants on passers-by from upstairs windows, putting ornaments down the lavatory, 'making waterfalls' by putting the plug in and turning on both taps in upstairs basins, climbing the garden gate and running off, getting up at 4 am and taking the house apart, are the types of behaviour that *have* to be *effectively* prevented. Try to keep major rows to really important taboos however.

If you have had a particularly noisy session, it is sometimes as well to explain to your neighbour what the problem was. Otherwise an extra-sympathetic smile and head-pat from the person next door (accompanied by a glare in the mother's direction) may undo all the good that the confrontation has just done!

The hyperactive child is very quick to pick up the nuances of 'poor little chap – his mother's very tough on him' that are frequently inspired by the rather appealing little face! But a hyperactive child whose confidence in his mother is undermined in this way has a double problem.

Be confident in how you are handling him, and share this confidence with your neighbour. Ask what *they* would do if *their* child got out of bed, climbed on the roof and started throwing stones down! Explain what you can – and then forget what they refuse to understand!

Sympathy from older people, who brought up families in an age before polluted crops, water, air, and junk foods brought the problem of hyperactivity, may be scant at first. Enlightenment may come, however, as the child improves! 'I didn't believe a word of what you were telling me at first, but he is so much better since he came off additives, I'm beginning to think there must be something in it', is music to the ears of a hard-pressed parent!

Resist, however, the temptation to complain about him more than is necessary to explain specific situations – and always try to keep your attitude positive and constructive: 'He will be better in a few weeks when we have cleansed his lead out', 'He's better in the summer, so we're having the gas boiler moved outside.' It is all too easy to be labelled 'that dreary mother with that ghastly little kid!'

While he is still very hyperactive it is best to avoid crowds and large gatherings where he is likely to be a pain to all present. If he cannot sit through prize-giving, a family wedding, the school play, or queue for the pleasure boats without fidgeting, grizzling or causing exasperation all round, it is as well to abandon such exercises for this year, or see if Granny will have him for the afternoon! Things will be better next year when the treatment has had time to take effect.

Some demands, however, must be made in the normal course of family life and when restraints necessarily arise, it is important to blame the *behaviour* and not the *child*, e.g. 'People don't do things like that' or 'That's a very naughty thing to do', rather than '*You* are a very naughty boy'. *He* is good; you and he are on the same side. *Bad temper, grabbing food, running away, hitting a friend* is naughty. *He*, being a good boy, mustn't do naughty things like that. You and he (the unit) don't do things like that. This message will take a long time to sink in, but in the end, you triumph together. He is your son and you love one another.

As the hyperactivity abates (and it may only take weeks to see a significant degree of improvement) more demands can be made. Point out how 'grown up' he is becoming and let his life become more complicated, a little at a time: 'You put on your socks and vest and I will help you with the rest'; 'You do three more spoonsful and then I will feed you'.

Tell other people how good and helpful he is being *in front* of him, and do not comment at all the days he backslides.

He will have to learn to do small household chores, to wait his turn with others, to *lose* at games and to develop skills requiring patience and dexterity. All of this is much harder for the hyperactive child than for the normal child, even after treatment, as he will have a big developmental backlog to make up. Maximum help should be given in the home, where his difficulties are understood, and all the family should remind him of chores, get him to put away toys, play games with him and *win* them, talk to him, help him accept it isn't his turn to choose the television programme, and generally give him as much 'life experience' as they can in his own home. Nowhere else will so much trouble be taken, so much understanding be shown, so much tolerance but firmness be exerted with even temper.

When he has improved noticeably, it is worth going to see his teacher, pointing out how much he has improved (and why!) and discussing his management with her. 'He will take turns now, if you are firm, and his speech is clearer. He will stop fidgeting if he is reminded, but we still need to touch his arm to get his attention when we speak to him . . .' The more you can communicate with the school, the better the cooperation will be, but sometimes the attitudes are too entrenched to make this possible. Transfer to a school where the attitude is more sympathetic to hyperactivity might be a solution in some cases. Try to remember though, when communicating with teachers and headmasters, what a pain he must be in a class of twenty! He may set other children off, or disturb or alienate them. Just imagine what having twenty of him would be like!

Finally, what about the parents themselves? Being the parents of a hyperactive child must be one of the most exacting jobs the world has ever thrown up. You have to be constantly vigilant and aware of the danger he may be to himself and others, day and night. Your emotional responses, usually so finely-tuned to your own child, are constantly scrambled by the atypical responses of the hyperactive child. Being constantly on the receiving end of temper or constantly apparently ignored, means your own reactions have to be exaggerated and emphasized every time you need to communicate, and with the hyper-active child, you have to communicate about once a minute.

But help is at hand. Parents of hyperactive children unite! Unite with each other and vow you are going to see your children back to normal in the next few years, come what may.

Unite with other parents who are lonely, harassed and confused, and isolated.

Unite with groups like HACSG who need help to spread the word. Write to Government ministers, headmasters, food manufacturers, school caterers, etc. Don't demand the impossible but achieving things like custard-coloured custard (not pink!) should not be beyond us.

Unite with your children – follow their diet, it will help you too.

Ignore gossip and criticism (there may be lots) and try to educate all and sundry on the causes and care of hyperactive children.

6
THE WAY FORWARD –
PREVENTING HYPERACTIVITY

Many of you who read this book and do not have a hyperactive child of your own may wonder whether the effort involved in following the treatments we suggest is worth it. Few parents who have hyperactive children would. The day-to-day problems of coping with such a child are so much more arduous, the problems at school and fears for the future loom so large, that a little extra cooking and giving a few tablets each day amount to nothing seen in the light of the child's improvement.

The beauty of the natural health approach we recommend is that it can do no harm – in fact it can do the whole family good. So often we hear how a younger brother's bed-wetting has stopped, or a mother's migraines have disappeared since the whole family have switched to the new diet.

The health and happiness of the family can start to spiral upwards instead of downwards as the diet helps the hyperactive child, and therefore the parents, tensions lessen and the whole family benefits.

Prevention of Hyperactivity

Before conception
Can hyperactivity be prevented? We believe the answer is yes. The Foresight Association was formed in 1978 to combat disadvantage in child health by preparing men and women for parenthood by natural methods. It believes that:

1. Both parents should be on a good wholefood diet prior to conception.

2. Both parents should discontinue smoking well in advance of conception, as smoking in pregnancy correlates with hyperactivity in the baby after birth, premature birth, and deformity.

3. Both parents should avoid alcohol prior to conception (alcohol can damage sperm) and the mother for the duration of the pregnancy and during lactation, as alcohol squanders the B vitamins and some essential minerals. The deformities and mental retardation associated with foetal alcohol syndrome are now well-documented.

4. Women should come off the contraceptive pill at least six months before the intended pregnancy and use a barrier method of contraception instead.

5. The couple should try to make sure they are free from infections, allergic syndromes, heavy metal toxicities and trace mineral deficiencies well in advance of pregnancy. (There are now several clinics where Foresight consultants can give advice on this.)

By taking these precautions prior to conception, we believe we can substantially increase the chances of the pregnancy starting well.

Pregnancy and birth

As pointed out above, dietary precautions and avoidance of toxic and allergenic substances should continue throughout the pregnancy.

The birth itself should be as natural and drug-free as possible (a very high percentage of births can be totally drug-free) followed by demand-feeding of colostrum and breast-milk.

Breast-feeding

In most cases, the demand-fed baby will feed very frequently for the first four to six days – a little and often is the best way to prepare and develop the immature digestive tract. After the first week, times between feeds should increase as the mother's milk becomes more plentiful.

For the mother a good varied diet, rich in unsaturated fats and vitamins and minerals, is the best way to promote a sufficient supply of good quality milk. Talk about 'resting' and 'relaxing' is all very fine, but except in the case of the first baby, it is seldom possible! Fear of being unable to relax as often as the experts prescribe may inhibit milk flow; as may assurances that 'if you worry your milk will go'. If the milk supply is going, it is due to insufficient nutrients – that is *why* the mother is worrying! If she eats well, takes vitamin and mineral supplements, puts the baby to the breast when he cries, the milk will flow in.

Where the mother is taking a good diet and sensible supplementation, separate vitamin supplements for the baby should not be necessary. Her breast-milk should be of sufficiently good quality to alleviate the need to give the baby fish-liver oils, rosehip syrup, etc. Giving breast-milk alone often prevents the early allergic syndromes. Some breast-fed babies have attacks of colic (crying and pulling up their legs) if the mother is drinking cow's milk. Some studies have shown that they are much more settled if their mother gives up drinking cow's milk and avoids cow products in general. This is well worth trying if the child is unsettled. Water is the best drink for nursing mothers.

Mixed feeding

With breast-feeding going well, mixed feeding can probably be postponed until about seventeen to twenty weeks – except in the case of the unusually large and hearty baby who may be ready for solids from about fifteen weeks.

The first tastes should be of very finely sieved foods, just a teaspoonful in the first instance. Only one new food should be given on each day, and if the food appears not to suit him, it should be *discontinued immediately* and not reintroduced for some months.

Little helpings should be worked up a teaspoonful at a time; the child should not be pressed to eat more than he needs. Very small amounts at two or three feeds will be better than one large meal. By six months, he may be taking a little baby rice at breakfast, with a teaspoonful of egg yolk; a few teaspoonsful of bone broth with sieved vegetables for lunch; a few teaspoonsful of sieved fruit for tea, followed each time by a plentiful breast-feed. Quantities should be very gradually increased as his enthusiasm for the food grows.

Different cereals can be introduced for breakfast, with a little helping of fruit or a drink of fruit juice, with egg yolk on alternate days. At lunch time, brain or pounded chicken, liver or fish, can be added to the strained vegetables and broth. Until at least eight months, breast-milk will remain the optional second course. At supper time, rusk soaked in milk or milk pudding can be given with mashed banana or sieved fruit, raw or stewed. Very gradually, a little at a time, items from the family meal can be added in, mashed, sieved or blended.

Once he is about nine to twelve months old, he will be able to sit happily in a high chair and join in family meals.

Lumpy food should not be given to the child before he is ready to chew it up. Giving him adult foods a few months too soon, so that large lumps of indigestible substances arrive in his stomach and cause acidity and colic is a frequent source of night screaming, skin rashes, irritability, diarrhoea and other allergic syndromes. He may not become a dab hand at chewing until he has cut the molars that come through at about 18 months, and many children need their meat shredded up until they have cut their two-year-old molars

Feeding fresh, finely sieved or mashed foods, in very small amounts at first, while continuing to breast-feed four to five times a day, is the best way to avoid setting up any adverse reaction – be it allergy, intolerance or sensitivity.

If a food 'does not suit him' – i.e., produces crying (pain), diarrhoea, nappy rash, other skin rashes, weeping cradle-cap, running nose, wheezing, coughing or other adverse symptoms, this should *not* be ignored. He is not having a 'temper tantrum', it is not 'just one of those things', he is having an allergic reaction. *The warning signs should not be ignored.*

To keep pushing a food into a child if it does not suit him, not only makes for an unhappy, grizzly, baby, it may make for a sickly, hyperactive child for years to come. Letting him thrive on foods that suit him and will help him to build up a good constitution, and later he may well be able to tolerate a wide variety of foods.

A sleepless night with a child when he is not actively teething or suffering from an infection needs investigation. What did he eat the previous day? The answer should be written down – if necessary at two in the morning – so it can be checked if it recurs. This way allergies can be spotted and eliminated right from the outset and many sleepless nights avoided for all the family.

If despite all efforts sleep patterns are poor, and appetite and temperament unreliable, it may be worth having a hair analysis as soon as he has enough hair. Meanwhile bottled or filtered water may help, as may avoiding areas of crowded traffic. The child should be kept away from cigarette smoke and his meals should not be prepared in aluminium saucepans.

These are some of the practical, day-to-day ways we may be able to avoid hyperactivity in our children. On a more long-term basis we can join – or form – groups which are trying to eliminate some of the dangers from our environment, be it lead in petrol or colouring in food.

But above all we need to spread the word – books in the recommended reading list will give an insight into the work we are doing. It is only fair to the next generation of children that we spread this knowledge before they are conceived – we could make the families, schools, and above all the *children* of the future so much happier.

Appendix 1
SPECIAL DIETS

The following diets have been used by parents of hyperactive children and found to be helpful.

The Feingold Food Programme

This food programme was devised by the late Dr Ben Feingold in the USA. On p.109 we give excerpts from letters we have had from parents who have used it with their hyperactive children in this country.

The background
Quoted from 'Food additives, the Feingold Diet and Hyperactivity'.

Elimination diets and specific testing suggest that food additives may be a factor in many cases of childhood hyperactivity. Dr Ben F. Feingold of Kaiser-Permanente Medical Center has reduced hyperactivity in children by placing them on a diet free of salicylates, artificial flavours and colours. Dr Feingold investigated adverse reactions to drugs and food additives, all low-molecular weight compounds. He found that aspirin (acetylsalicylic acid) and the salicylates in foods and some synthetic flavours cause allergic reactions in sensitive people. When other researchers reported that the commonly-used food dye tartrazine (FD and C yellow 5) caused reactions in aspirin-sensitive patients, Feingold designed a diet free of all artificial flavours and colours, aspirin, and natural salicylates. The diet was initially prescribed for patients with itching, hives, skin rashes, anxiety, and asthma. When these allergic reactions and also the mental symptoms improved, Feingold began using the diet to treat hyperactive children! 50 per cent of the children put on the diet responded fully, while 70 per cent improved enough to be taken off drugs.

Several research studies indicate that the Feingold diet may be an effective treatment for hyperactivity. In America, the Government is now encouraging further research on the Feingold Diet at the University of Wisconsin. Drs Clyde Hawley and Robert E. Buckley have developed a test using official food dyes that a doctor can use to determine food-dye sensitivity in children. Drs Cook and Woodhill treated fifteen hyperactive children with the Feingold Diet; of these ten improved, and three may have improved according to the parents. Relapses occurred and the young patients became more hyperactive when the forbidden foods were eaten.

How does the Feingold Diet correlate with the high lead, copper and low zinc findings?

Salicylates, benzoates, and tartrazine and chelating agents will grab onto the esential trace elements and interfere with their absorption. Of the three, the most active is probably the yellow dye tartrazine and the least active is the benzoate molecule. The intestinal contents contain partially-digested food with various concentrations of copper, zinc, iron, lead, calcium, and magnesium. Grains contain phytate which decreases the absorption of zinc because phytate is a known chelating agent. These chelating agents are more specific for some metals than for others. Therefore the absorption of copper and lead could be increased by salicylates and tartrazine while the absorption of zinc could be decreased. Orotic acid in milk whey is also a chelating agent and therefore may be a factor in hyperactivity. These additives could thereby increase hyperactivity in children who have a high level of lead and copper in their food and drink and a low level of zinc and calcium. This is a testable hypothesis which would take much of the mystery out of the food allergy story.

Since salicylates and food additives evidently do enhance some types of hyperactivity, placing a child on the Feingold Diet might relieve the condition and certainly would do no harm. The mode of action of the dyes and salicylates may be owing to the chemical chelating effect which these compounds have on trace elements.[1]

How to begin

1. Read with care everything you can on the Feingold food programme, including Dr Feingold's book *Why Your Child is Hyperactive*.

2. Keep a diet diary, noting everything the individual eats and drinks, along with a side-by-side record of behaviour and sleep patterns, so that these can be compared. This record should be kept even after success with the programme is achieved. In the event of an unfavourable reaction, the diet record makes it easy to determine which food caused the problem.

3. The greatest success is observed when the entire family adheres to the programme. This requires your commitment and support of all family members. When the prohibited foods are not present in the house, temptation and the risk of infractions are reduced. The all-out effort by all family members serves as an added incentive to the child. Many families have found that the eliminations of the non-essential additives often benefits other members of the family as well, both children and adults.

4. This food programme must be adhered to 100 per cent. Compliance of 90 per cent does not yield a 90 per cent improvement, but rather leads to disappointment. A single bite or sip can lead to a reaction that may last for 72 hours.

5. Reading food labels is very important. However, you should realize that some labels can be misleading and regulations are far too many to quote individually here. It is best not to buy anything which says it contains 'preservatives', 'colour' or 'flavouring' unless it is on the 'safe' list. 'Natural colouring', 'natural flavouring' should be all right.

6. The key is to be selective in the grocery store. Once the food is in the house it is too late to determine if it is 'safe'. It is hard to tell a child 'no' to something he already has in his hands.

7. Please let bakers, butchers, food manufacturers know that you want pure non-additive foods for your family. When asking about food, it is not enough to say 'Is it all natural?' You will get a more helpful response if you are specific: 'Is it made with real or imitation vanilla? Are there any preservatives in it?' etc.

8. *Away from home* As it is very important that your child adheres to the diet, it is advisable to send a packed lunch for school. If the headteacher will not agree, please let us know. Your doctor or health visitor may help here. Most headteachers are very cooperative, once they understand the situation. If your child is bothered by refusing 'treats' when away from home suggest this response: 'Thank you, but I am sensitive to artificial colours and flavours'. Some children find it easier to say 'I'm allergic' (although this sensitivity is not allergy according to the medical definition of allergy). Usually this approach will elicit a sympathetic response on the part of his friends, whereas 'I'm on a diet' may prompt ridicule. When there is a birthday party most

hostesses will not be insulted if you telephone ahead and explain the difficulty, ask what is on the menu and send substitutions. In time he may report back that the mother of the birthday-child is going to join the 'programme' because so many brought their own food and drink!

9. *Medicines* When drugs have been prescribed a physician should be notified before making any changes in the medication. Since many drugs are synthetically coloured and flavoured, ask your physician or pharmacist to prescribe non-coloured/flavoured drugs and medicines. Behaviour-modifying drugs, aside from containing colour and flavouring, have been known to have long-lasting residual effects. If your child has been on these drugs, it may be necessary to wait longer to see the desired effect of the diet.

General comments taken from responses to the HACSG's questionnaire on the Feingold food programme

The diet is a god-send.

Indirectly the whole family has benefitted from a calmer child who sleeps better.

We can live as a normal family, instead of a front-line fighting force.

The diet has turned J into a delightful child whom other children seek out, and it has saved our sanity.

We all feel better healthwise.

Now we are all on the 'diet' I have not had one migraine since being on it and we all seem that much fitter.

Child seems calmer and I feel better and have had less migraines.

Calmer child makes life both inside and outside the house more pleasant for all. Friends have commented how much calmer S is.

C is now a normal happy child on the diet and if given food he is 'allergic' to, the reaction is noticeable to anyone.

Child growing tall and well – healthy and bright-eyed.

Family life is less fraught now . . .

Child much improved – discharged from doctor and I have had no more of the chest infections I used to have.

Our lives have completely changed since the diet – it was like a nightmare before.

The atmosphere in our home is now more relaxed.

I firmly believe the diet has worked for my son, I only wish I had used it sooner.

The diet has helped immensely, but I think that a lot of the problems developed because of his being hyperactive so long, these will take some time to sort out, but this is now possible because he is much calmer and more cooperative (boy aged 8 years).

Whole family on the diet – other children are much healthier too.

We are healthier and more relaxed as a result of the diet and we consequently enjoy life more and achieve more.

I wish the medical profession would take more notice of it.

All have better health and tempers.

Health of whole family improved – sinusitis, eczema, mouth ulcers have gone.

General improvement in health and growth but greatest improvement in temperament after giving vitamin B.

Child has not needed any *drugs* since the diet took effect after three to four weeks.

Without the diet I think we would have all gone round the bend.

Surprised at the amount of food additives, colouring, etc. in today's food.

This list could be repeated over and over again.

Extracts from letters from mothers of hyperactive children who have been using the Feingold Diet. March 1978

Since reading your article we have dropped all mono-sodium glutamate from his diet and all fruit juices and in 3 weeks we can see an improvement – we have had 2 nights of undisturbed sleep and to me and my husband that is heaven – also his general outlook is better – he doesn't cry all the time and his nightmares and sleepwalking are much better.
(Baby 14 months old.)

Before she was put on the diet she was very excitable and overactive; she had many tantrums often 1 or 2 a day and had excessive crying sessions. She was unhappy and very bad tempered, her power of concentration was poor and her speech was bad, very muddled – she has to attend speech therapy. Since starting the diet there have been vast improvements. Gone are the daily tantrums and excessive crying bouts. She has definitely slowed down to a much more normal pace and her speech has started to improve rapidly . . . she is now most definitely a much happier little girl. And my husband and myself and family are absolutely thrilled with the most outstanding results to date.
(Girl aged 5.)

I have now had baby on the diet for just over two weeks. Even friends who don't see him often have commented

on the difference, so I really believe this is what has been the trouble. After crying tears of relief and remorse for all the times I've screamed 'for God's sake shut up'. I am now taking a real joy and pride in my lovely son instead of loving him with gritted teeth... Last week he *actually slept* on 3 separate days till 5.30-6 am and settled again after a drink. His concentration has improved a thousandfold ... I am so enthusiastic over this I would help anyone. I am sure that children like this are much more likely to be battered as time and time again friends and relatives have said 'if he were theirs they just don't know how they'd cope'. I was reaching breaking point as the smacks were getting harder and more frequent, when suddenly I read your article . . .
(Boy 1 year old.)

The diet has been duplicated and will be available at the weekly clinic. I have also given copies to other playgroup mothers. As yet it has been too early to see if they have noticed any change. It is strange but we all just thought our children were awkward . . . my son's sleeping habits have definitely improved... before it used to be a couple of hours here, an hour there - now he will go to sleep and have 5 hours at a stretch, play a while and then have another hour; this alone means a great deal to my husband and I. I believe he is improving behaviourwise. His eating is very spasmodic but at least four times since starting the diet he has sat down at the meal table and eaten a proper meal . . . A real treat for us!
(Small boy.)

I am writing to thank you for Dr Feingold's diet sheet. I read of your Group in the *Mother* magazine, and although my son is not hyperactive he does suffer from hayfever - or at least he did!

I am overjoyed at his response to the diet and my husband (who suffers from the same complaint) on seeing his son's obvious improvement, started the diet too. Since then neither of them has needed anti-histamine, mentholatum or eye drops, all of which were a daily necessity.

I am very grateful and inform people daily of the benefits!

(Mother from West Midlands)

Eight months ago I put my son on the diet. We now have a healthy, contented child who I have not had to take to the doctors for 6 months. It used to be six weeks. I would be than willing to give any assistance if required to the local contact.

(Mother of small 5-year-old.)

The 'Caveman' diet

This diet was devised by Dr Elizabeth Lodge-Rees of California. It is essentially an 'elimination' diet which is used first to identify foods which may produce a bad reaction and then to rebuild a healthy diet. The name 'Caveman' emphasizes the need to eliminate modern processed foods. As we understand it, the basic principles are:

1. Determine which foods we use today would have been used before frozen or processed foods.

2. Accept that the bad effects of previous diet may take four to five weeks to be eliminated from the body.

3. Sugar and flour-based products are *out* (i.e., sweets, ice cream, biscuits, cakes, puddings).

4. Most cereal-based foods are *out* (i.e., white flour, breakfast cereals, including cornflakes, rice) unless they are complete, i.e., wholemeal flour, brown rice, possibly oatmeal (although with some children these may still be suspect).

5. Milk and dairy foods (butter, cream, cheese) are also suspect – as is margarine.

6. Added salt should only be rock or sea-salt as proprietary brands frequently have supplements or additives to make them free-running.

7. Only *water* should be drunk – *no* tea, coffee, chocolate or malted drinks, milk or squash.

Suggestions for a Gluten-free, Milk-free Diet

Try to vary the dishes every day.

Cooked breakfast
Bacon, egg, kidney, fish, with sautéed potato. Tomato, prunes, banana and mushrooms can all be fried with bacon.

Kedgeree made with herring, mackerel or sardine, rice bicarbonate of soda as a rising agent – baking powders mackerel or sardines; tuna, sardines or smoked mackerel

Omelettes can be filled with almost anything – mushrooms, ham, onion, chopped herbs such as chives (small amount).

Eggs can be beaten up in mashed potato and fried to make flat yellow things! Nice with *Marmite*. (No milk in mash.)

Cold sardines and tuna fish with tomato.

Tea with lemon, or juice.

Goats' or soy milk if tolerated. Goats' milk or soy milk (Plamilk) can be made into milkshakes with banana or any soft fruit* and honey. Also nice with peanut butter, egg and honey.

Raw fruit

Lunch
Any fresh meat, fish, poultry or offal and two, or three vegetables. Gravy must be made with cornflour. Mix first with cold water then add boiling water, meat juice or Marmite, or better still, bone jelly!

Raw or stewed fruit. Apple snow. Jelly, home-made from fruit juice and gelatine.

If goats' or soy milk tolerated, milk puddings with rice, ground rice, sago, cornflour, custard made with honey. Ice cream made with goats' milk, eggs and honey.

Tea/supper

Soups
A nice hot soup can be made by boiling up bones and making jelly and then adding peas, beans, lentils (soaked overnight), also tomato, carrot, leek, onion, mushroom, potato, etc.

Salads
Salads can be made of raw fruit* and vegetables, e.g. lettuce, endive, cucumber, apple, date, beetroot, carrot, tomato, cold cooked potato, white shredded cabbage etc., with dressing. Baked or fried potato.

Ham, sardine, tuna fish, tongue, corned beef, hard-boiled egg, prawns, smoked mackerel etc. can accompany the salad.

Puddings
Goats' milk or soy milkshake or juice. Cakes and biscuits made from potato flour and whey-free margarine. Use bicarbonate of soda as a raising agent – baking powders contain gluten.

Farmer's Wife apple and orange juice are additive free, other juices can be made at home. Dried fruit, sultanas, raisins, etc. and nuts.

Suggestions for a Gluten-free, Milk-free, Egg-free Diet

Breakfast

Bacon with kidney, liver, mushrooms, tomatoes, bananas, prunes, apple rings or sautéed potatoes.

Fish: plain baked or grilled; kedgeree can be made with rice and sweetcorn, from smoked haddock, smoked makckerel or sardines; tuna, sardines or smoked mackerel can be eaten cold with bean shoots.

Raw fruit and fruit juices.

Goats' or soy milk, if tolerated. Milkshakes made with banana or any soft fruit and honey. Also nice with peanut butter, or just plain honey.

Lunch

Any fresh meat, fish, poultry or offal, with two or three vegetables, potato or rice. Gravies or sauces must be thickened with arrowroot, cornflour or split-pea flour.

Raw or stewed fruit. If goats' or soy milk tolerated, puddings can be made with plain, flaked or ground rice, sago, cornflour or gluten-free semolina (obtainable from Boots).

Supper

Soups

Bone broth made from bone jelly. Thicken with peas, beans, lentils, split-pea flour or potato. Add meat scraps and vegetables such as carrots, leeks, onions, mushrooms, swedes, beets, etc.

Salads

Any raw fruit* and vegetable such as lettuce, endive, cucumber, apple, date, beet, carrot, tomato, coleslaw, cress, sprouted seeds, etc. Dressing made with safflower oil, cider vinegar* and honey. Baked or boiled potato.

Sardine, tuna, cold meats, prawns, cold fish, etc.

Puddings
Goat or soy milkshake. Juice.

Dried fruits: sultanas, raisins, pears, apricots, peaches.
Nuts: walnuts, almonds, brazils, cashews.

Books on Special Diets

The following books should be available from health
food stores. If not, order directly from: Roberts Publications, Larkhall Laboratories, 225 Putney Bridge Road,
London SW15 2PY.

GREER, R. (1977) *The Extraordinary Kitchen Notebook*
Bunterbird
A cookery book for food allergies based on the recipes
(gluten-free, egg-free, refined-sugar-free and milk-free)
she used to rehabilitate her husband to full health from
life in a wheelchair. Over a hundred attractive, original
recipes (for children and adults) based on wholefood
principles.

GREER, R. (1977) *Fruit and Vegetables in Particular* Bunterbird
A sequel to *The Extraordinary Kitchen Notebook* based on the
same dietary restrictions but exclusively vegetarian/
vegan too. Over a hundred more recipes to increase
variety even more for the food-sensitive patient.

GREER, R. (1978) *The First Clinical Ecology Cookbook*
Bunterbird
Over a hundred more original recipes based on the same
general dietary restrictions as the two previous books but
this time with further refinement. Some food allergy
sufferers are sensitive to items included after the overall
restrictions so Rita has designed a range of symbols which
indicate the further eliminations achieved by each recipe.
A real boon for the very allergic patient.

GREER, R. and WOODWARD, R. (1982) *Food Allergy: A Practical Easy Guide* Roberts Publications
This concise book helps you to determine whether you are really a food allergic or just suffering from poor nutrition. Wholefood nutrition, correct vitamin and mineral supplementation for health, warnings about the seven modern diet dangers are included before a full discussion of food allergy – symptoms and treatment, examples of detection and control diets. An up-to-date list of treatment and advice centres is given.

HILLS, C. H. (1973) *Good Food Gluten-Free* Roberts Publications
The classic book which started the exposure of the so-called 'gluten-free foods' which were not only not genuine but virtually useless as nutritious foods. Explains good nutrition for the coeliac or wheat sensitive (allergic) patient (child or adult) in simple terms backed with hundreds of recipes.

HILLS, C. H. (1978) *Good Food, Grain-Free, Milk-Free* Roberts Publications
A sequel to *Good Food, Gluten-Free* based on the same wholefood diet principles but eliminating all grains (wheat, rye, barley, oats, rice and maize) as well as all milk products. Easy to follow and plenty of nutritious recipes and suggestions for substitute foods meeting the strict requirements of this diet.

Appendix 2
THE HYPERACTIVE CHILDREN'S SUPPORT GROUP[1]

The Hyperactive Children's Support Group was founded in November 1977 and grew into a national association almost overnight. It was accorded charitable status in May 1979.

The aims of the Group are 'to help and support hyperactive children and their parents; to conduct research and promote investigation into the incidence of hyperactivity in the UK – its causes and treatments; and to disseminate information concerning this condition'.

Many children are hyperactive (HA) from birth (they are often HA in utero); they are restless, fidgety, sleep perhaps three to four hours out of 24 and cry almost incessantly. They will not feed properly, whether breast or bottle fed, and may also suffer from asthma and eczema. The mother is completely bewildered by this, especially if it is her first baby – no amount of nursing, cuddling, or comforting will pacify such a child.

As these children grow older this hyperactive behaviour is accentuated – they seem in a state of perpetual motion, which makes them extremely accident prone. Although a high IQ is possible, many HA children experience difficulty in learning; speech can be a problem, and often balance is poor, with extreme clumsiness. They are prone to cot-rocking and head banging; their behaviour is unpredictable and disruptive; they are easily excitable and cry often; they are unable to sit still for more than a few minutes at a time; coordination and concentration are very poor.

[1] Adapted from *Health Visitor*, January 1980.

They are poor sleepers and eaters. There is often a history of headaches, catarrh, asthma, hay fever, and other respiratory complaints; and boys are more likely to be affected than girls. Another strange symptom which has emerged from many letters from mothers is that almost all HA children suffer from abnormal thirst.

We believe that a connection may exist between baby battering and hyperactivity, since in many cases the condition is not diagnosed and most parents have never heard of hyperactivity.

Mothers have written to say that they feel 'loners' and social outcasts. They feel their children create such havoc wherever they go that they are not welcome in playgroups, nursery school, shops, friends' or relatives' homes. A simple shopping trip takes on nightmarish qualities.

Many of these babies and children are prescribed a succession of drugs to try and control this behaviour, but even in adult dosage, drugs give poor results.

My own son Miles was born hyperactive and for six long years we battled with his exhausting behaviour; the only treatment offered was a succession of drugs none of which seemed very effective. Then quite by chance I heard about a diet which Dr Ben Feingold (Chief Emeritus, Department of Allergy, Kaiser Permanents Medical Centre, San Francisco) had formulated from his researches as an allergist. I lost no time in sending for this and after *four days* of starting Miles on it he was a changed child – he actually slept the night, which in itself was a small miracle.

The diet is a very simple one. It is designed to eliminate as far as possible synthetic chemical additives from a person's diet, i.e. colours, flavours, MSG, BHA, BHT and others; and for the first four to six weeks only certain fruits and vegetables which contain natural salicylates; salicylates are 'aspirin like' chemicals to which HA children are often sensitive. Gradually the suspect fruits can be reintroduced and if no adverse response is noted they can be added to the daily menus.

Miles responded well to the diet; he became much calmer and was able to sit at the table to eat a proper meal; he learnt to read quite quickly, was much less disruptive at school, and altogether he is a much happier little boy.

My health visitor was so astounded at the change in Miles that she recommended the diet to other mothers who were experiencing difficulties with their children: before long it was obvious that I would not be able to cope single-handed with all the enquiries which came pouring in and several kind friends helped me form the Group.

I adapted the Feingold diet to English foods and we now have a basic 'diet booklet', comprising an explanatory letter, information and book list, permitted/non permitted foods list, 'safe' shopping guide and ideas for meals, which we think helps mothers when first beginning the diet.

Membership is on an annual basis, with three newsletters to keep members up-to-date on the latest information which comes to us from various sources, items on research, recipes, additions to the 'safe' foods guide, etc.

The diet is really a very healthy one, and most mothers find it easier to keep the whole family on it, rather than having 'different' food in the house. Any infraction of the diet by the child may have serious consequences with a reversion to behaviour disturbances.

To date we have had well over 60,000 letters from distraught parents which may give a clue to the size of the problem. We are pleased to say that very many HA children have shown good improvements on this diet, so much so in some cases that perhaps they have not had to be sent to a 'special' school; other traumatic experiences have been avoided.

Local Groups

We have over 130 groups in the UK and one in Guernsey,

all started by grateful mothers. These are proving extremely helpful, as mothers are able to share experiences and make new friends who understand and sympathise. New members are put in touch with their local group (or if there isn't one they are encouraged to begin one). The Groups hold informal meetings and we understand many fathers attend these; some have had money-raising events for our Research Fund; no doubt they will go from strength to strength.

Mothers are finding that with the lifting of their burden of guilt (they are often accused of being the cause of their child's hyperactivity, that they have mismanaged the child, etc.), they have much more confidence in themselves; with a happier mother and calmer child, families are really beginning to enjoy being a family.

We are also in correspondence with Australian, American and Canadian hyperactive support groups.

Other Causes

There are other causes of HA such as hypoglycaemia, milk allergy, food allergies, nutritional deficiency and possibly environmental pollution. However, we feel that the Feingold diet is something which mothers may try for themselves; it contains no drugs, is based on simple fresh foods, and is entirely beneficial. Our advice to mothers is to try the diet for two to three months and if you need help we can advise further.

Ideally, of course, every HA child should have a thorough examination and specialist diagnosis so that the causes can be pinpointed; however, until this handicap is widely known, this is not always possible.

Research

An important aim is research. It is not known for certain how many HA children and adolescents there are in the

UK for instance; our Group hope to be able to help with this.

Mothers of some of our first 'better children' completed a questionnaire which has been used as a basis for research at Surrey University. Research is also being carried out into food allergies and behavioural disturbances. Now that we are a Charity, we hope to be able to raise funds for further research into this soul destroying handicap.

We are anxious to keep in touch with as many members of the medical profession, educationists etc. as possible; every scrap of information and feedback is essential in the research.

The Government Food Additives and Contaminants Committee have recently recommended, in three separate reviews, the following bans:

Colourings 21 March 1979 (press notice)
Recommended that colours should no longer be permitted for use in foods described either directly or by implication as being especially prepared for infants and young children.

The recommendation regarding colouring matter in infants and young children has not yet been legislated for . . . A letter to HACSG in December 1979 said: 'the majority of such foods sold in the U.K. do not contain added colour, but consideration is being given to implementing the Committee's recommendation . . .'

Nitrites and Nitrates
Legislation (similar to above conditions) enacted in 'Preservatives in Food Regulations' Amendment No.15, February 1982.

Flavour Modifiers
Legislation (similar to above) enacted in Miscellaneous Additives in Food Regulations No.14, 1983.

Pregnancy

We would ask that special help and advice be given to mothers-to-be so that they understand the *great importance* of good nutrition for themselves and their baby from the beginning of pregnancy. We urge avoidance of foods containing the previously mentioned chemical additives. We recommend the use of as few tinned foods as possible (tins are sealed with lead and recent research has shown that much tinned food has above the allowed limit of cadmium.)

Diet Allowance

This is only for families (or single parents) on state supplementary benefit. And you need the support of your doctor when applying.

Attendance Allowance

Parents of hyperactive children *are eligible* to apply for this allowance. Form N 1205 from Social Security local offices.

Vulnerability of Very Young Infants

(WHO Food Additives Report 1971. Page 33, para. 4.1.) Very young infants are especially vulnerable to foreign chemicals because the mechanisms that provide protection against these substances are absent or not fully developed. Although the evidence for this derives mainly from studies with drugs rather than with food additives, it is likely that such very young infants are less efficient than older children in metabolizing some food additives and may therefore accumulate them to excessive levels. If this occurs at a time when sensitivity to toxic effects is critical because of the delicately balanced growth and different-iation processes, there may be deleterious consequences that may not appear until much later in the child's development. Very young infants may also differ from older children in relation to physiological barriers protecting sensitive tissues, such as the blood brain barrier or the protective barriers for retinal or lens tissue.

Conclusion

All we ask for is open minds on the subject of the dietary approach to this multiple handicap. We are pleased to report that many doctors are considering this as an alternative to drug therapy, especially when they have seen for themselves the results in previously intransigent hyperactivity.

We have letters from mothers saying that cases of severe migraine, asthma, eczema, epilepsy, dyslexia, and recently a case of severe mental handicap, have responded to this food programme, as the Americans now call it.

Information About the Group

First year membership is £3.00, renewal £5.00. For Single Parent Families or those on Social benefit there is a special rate.

Members are entitled to all newsletters issued during the year, contact with local group, free advice and help (as far as we are able). Access to research information. Free copy of research hypothesis and parents' notes on evening primrose oil.

Members joining from September to December each year, do not need to renew payment until the *following* December/January.

Diet Booklet. This costs £2.00 and includes full details of the Feingold diet, EEC numbers of colourings to be avoided, 'safe' foods guide, local contacts and groups. Also a resumé of our research hypothesis, helpful reading list, notes on allergies and hair analysis, and many other items of information.

All correspondence to The Secretary, Sally Bunday, 59 Meadowside, Angmering, West Sussex, BN16 4BW.

Be sure to send a S.A.E. if you need information etc. as we are a voluntary group, and our funds are limited.

If a copy of the Diet Booklet only is required, please mark your envelope **Diet Please**.

USEFUL ADDRESSES

Association for Children with Learning Difficulties Quirral House, Pitch Place, Thursley, Godalming, Surrey.

CALIP *(Campaign Against Lead in Petrol)* 68 Dora Road, London SW19 7HH.

Cantassium Company, 225 Putney Bridge Road, London SW15 2PY.

CLEAR *(The Campaign for Lead Free Air)* 2 Northdown Street, London N1 9BG.

Conservation Society 12a Guildford Street, Chertsey, Surrey.

Foodwatch, High Acre, East Stour, Gillingham, Dorset SP8 5JR.

Foresight (The Association for the Promotion of Preconceptual Care) Mrs Peter Barnes, The Old Vicarage, Church Lane, Witley, Godalming, Surrey GU8 5PN.

The Henry Doubleday Research Association 32 Convent Road, Bocking, Braintree, Essex.

Hyperactive Children's Support Group 59 Meadowside, Angmering, Sussex.

G & G Vitamin Centre, 51 Railway Approach, East Grinstead, West Sussex RH19 1BT.

The McCarrison Society Pauline Atkin, 23 Stanley Court, Worcester Road, Sutton, Surrey.

The Organic Food Service Ashe, Churston Ferrers, Brixham, Devon, will provide addresses of places selling organically-grown food.

Sanity Marjorie Hall, 77 Moss Lane, Pinner, Middlesex HA5 3A6.

The Schizophrenia Association of Great Britain Mrs Gwynneth Hemmings, Llanfair Hall, Caernavon, Gwynned, Wales.

Mayrei Water Filters, 'La Source de Vie', P.O. Box 66, Chichester, Sussex.

FURTHER RECOMMENDED READING

CRAWFORD, M. and S. (1972) *What We Eat Today* Neville Spearman.

CROOK, W. G. *Tracking Down Hidden Food Allergies.*

DAVIS, A. (1971) *Let's Eat Right to Keep Fit* Allen and Unwin.

EAGLE, R. (1979) *Eating and Allergy*, Futura Publications.

ELAM, D. (1979) *Building Better Babies.*

FEINGOLD, B. *Why Your Child is Hyperactive* Random House.

GOLAS, N. (1969) *Management of Complex Allergies* New England Foundation of Allergic and Environmental Diseases, 3 Brush Street, Norwalk, Connecticut 06850, USA.

HUNTER, B. T. (1972) *The Natural Foods Primer* Unwin.

MACKARNESS, R. (1980) *Chemical Victims* Pan.

NORWOOD, C. *At Highest Risk* McGraw Hill.

PFEIFFER, C. (1978) *Zinc and Other Micronutrients* Random House.

PRICE, W. (1945) *Nutrition and Physical Degeneration* Price Pottenger Foundation, PO Box 2614, La Mesa, California 92041.

SCHROEDER, H. (1975) *Trace Elements and Man* Devin-Adair, Old Greenwich, Connecticut.

SCHROEDER, H. *The Poisons Around Us.*

WILLIAMS, R. *Nutrition Against Disease.*

WILLIAMS, R. *Nutrition in a Nutshell.*

INDEX